PILGRIM'S ROAD

Also by Bettina Selby:

Riding the Desert Trail
Riding to Jerusalem
Beyond Ararat
Riding the Mountains Down
The Fragile Islands
Riding North One Summer
Frail Dream of Timbuktu

PILGRIM'S ROAD

A Journey to Santiago de Compostela

Bettina Selby

LITTLE, BROWN AND COMPANY

A *Little, Brown* Book

First published in Great Britain
by Little, Brown and Company 1994

Copyright © Bettina Selby 1994

The moral right of the author has been asserted.

A CIP catalogue record for this book
is available from the British Library.

ISBN 0 316 90699 9

Typeset by Hewer Text Composition Services, Edinburgh
Printed and bound in Great Britain by
Clays Ltd, St Ives plc.

Little, Brown and Company (UK) Limited
Brettenham House
Lancaster Place
London WC2 7EN

For all who take the Santiago Road

Give me my scallop shell of quiet;
My staff of faith to walk upon;
My scrip of joy, immortal diet;
My bottle of salvation;
My gown of glory (hope's true gage)
And then I'll take my pilgrimage.

Sir Walter Raleigh

Contents

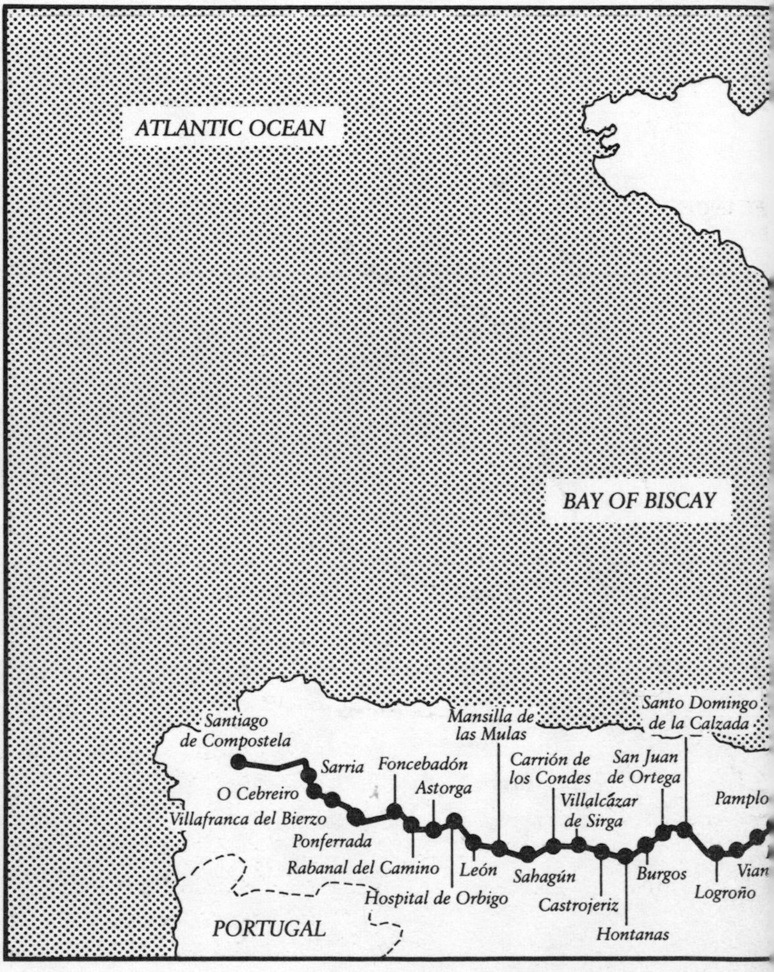

ATLANTIC OCEAN

BAY OF BISCAY

Santiago
de Compostela

Mansilla de
las Mulas

Santo Domingo
de la Calzada

Sarria   Foncebadón

Carrión de
los Condes

San Juan
de Ortega

O Cebreiro   Astorga

Villalcázar
de Sirga

Pamplo

Villafranca del Bierzo

Ponferrada

Rabanal del Camino   León

Sahagún   Burgos   Vian

Hospital de Orbigo

Castrojeriz

Logroño

PORTUGAL

Hontanas

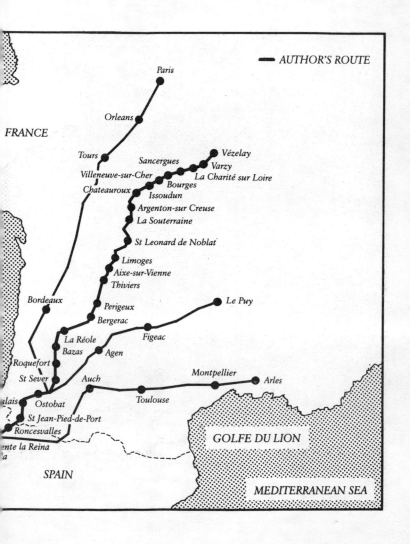

AUTHOR'S ROUTE

Paris

Orleans

FRANCE

Tours

Sancergues

Vézelay

Varzy

Villeneuve-sur-Cher

La Charité sur Loire

Chateauroux

Bourges

Issoudun

Argenton-sur Creuse

La Souterraine

St Leonard de Noblat

Limoges

Aixe-sur-Vienne

Thiviers

Bordeaux

Perigeux

Le Puy

Bergerac

La Réole

Figeac

Bazas

Agen

Roquefort

St Sever

Auch

Montpellier

Arles

'alais

Ostobat

Toulouse

St Jean-Pied-de-Port

Roncesvalles

GOLFE DU LION

ente la Reina

a

SPAIN

MEDITERRANEAN SEA

St James

1

The Way

We arrived at Vézelay on an evening in early April just as dusk was falling. Against the darkening sky the great church of La Madeleine rode the rolling plains of Burgundy like a galleon in full sail. Built to act as a magnet to draw men to it from afar, eight centuries later it had not lost its power. Tired though we were, we made straight up the hill before even considering a restorative drink or a place to stay. There was time that evening for only the briefest look at the astounding carving of the Christ in the narthex, and a glimpse of the huge arched spaces of the nave before the doors were locked for the night.

We found a room with the sisters in the nearby convent at the top of the steep, narrow street which leads down from the church, and which in fact is not a village street at all, but 'The Way', for every inch of this hill is charged with significance and rich in legend. However, we were content to leave further explorations until the morning, for after the thirteen-hour drive from the overnight ferry we wanted nothing more than to collapse into the large lumpy bed beneath the obligatory crucifix, and were asleep by nine.

The aged and battered 2CV known as the Red Toad – as much for its difficult but endearing nature, as for the bulbous headlamps and vaguely amphibious appearance – was parked outside the cathedral ready for my husband Peter's early morning return to England. My bicycle, which the Red Toad had transported to the start of the journey, was locked safely (as we wrongly assumed) in the convent's front hall, ready to set out in the opposite direction – southward to Santiago de Compostela.

Being a compulsive traveller, the idea of making a journey excites me whatever the time of year; but as Chaucer so rightly observed, an English April is like no other season for stirring the wanderlust. With the first delicate greening of black winter branches, buds breaking free in skeletal hedgerows, and infinitely small and tender shoots bravely pushing up out of the bare cold earth, a marvellous metamorphosis begins. Skies which have been grey for months are suddenly blue, and the air has a delicious new softness, full of heady scents recalling past delights. The earth, in the process of rediscovering itself, seems to call for a similar unfolding and expanding of the human heart, and the sense of freshness and renewal everywhere makes it almost unbearable to stay indoors.

So strong is this siren call of the awakening year that even in the traffic-choked centres of cities like London it makes itself heard; and lucky the traveller who has the freedom to give ear to it. Seasons and weather being so variable in our northern latitudes, however, and so seldom performing quite as expected, these seductive harbingers of spring came early in March the year I fastened a scallop shell to my panniers and set out to bicycle to the 'Field of the Star'.

The idea of journeying along the ancient medieval

pilgrim route to the shrine of St James the Apostle, patron saint of Spain, came about quite by chance. One day the morning's post brought me a card illustrated with a reproduction of an old map showing the four main pilgrim routes leading to Santiago de Compostela. It had been sent by a friend who had selected it quite at random, I learnt subsequently, but the timing could not have been more apt. Pilgrimage was so perfectly in keeping with the burgeoning year, and as it also coincided with the discovery that I had some two months unexpectedly clear of commitments, the idea took fire at once.

Most of my journeys seem to have come about by pure chance; a sudden enthusiasm that grew into a fully fledged ambition. Recently, however, I have begun to wonder if perhaps there isn't some sort of pattern to my wanderings, or, at the very least, a right time for making a particular journey. I was to ponder this thought often on the Road to Compostela.

All I knew about the St James or Jacobite pilgrimage was that Santiago was in Galicia, that mysterious Celtic region of north-western Spain, near Cape Finisterre – the end of the world – and an area I had long wanted to visit. When I looked up the route in the atlas, I found that it went through the sort of varied and rugged terrain I most enjoy, crossing several mountain ranges, including the Pyrenees. It also passed through a number of historic towns famous for their medieval treasures. In fact the whole way appeared to be studded with monasteries, Romanesque churches and romantic ruins, and pointed to an intriguing and challenging journey, though one very different from my usual adventures. Getting away from the beaten track is usually my goal, whereas this route had been trodden by millions of pilgrim feet, and even in an increasingly

3

materialistic world it had never completely fallen into disuse. The thought that so time-honoured a road was still followed today made it all the more intriguing. Within an hour of the postcard landing on my mat I had made up my mind to accept the challenge, and immediately set about making my preparations.

The first thing to decide upon was from which of the four traditional pilgrim starting places or assembly points, should I begin my journey. The most northerly of them, Paris, was convenient for those coming from Britain, Germany, the Low Countries and Northern France, and clearly would be the easiest for me. But its rallying place, the church of St Jacques de la Boucherie, has long since been torn down in the interests of road widening, and only its great square tower now remains. Besides, the route from Paris goes through Orléans, Tours, Poitiers and Bordeaux, towns already familiar to me; I had a hankering for fresh pastures.

The most southerly route, which served those coming up from Italy and the South of France, begins at Arles and goes through Montpelier and Toulouse. This attracted me far more, but again it was countryside that I had already travelled, and it would also mean an extra few hundred miles to reach the start of the journey.

Le Puy, on the western side of the Massif Central, was nearer, and had the distinction of being the starting place of the first recorded St James pilgrimage when, in 951, the Bishop of Le Puy led some of his faithful flock to Compostela and back again. I almost plumped for this tempting route through the Auvergne, which offered the additional delights of the medieval towns of Moissac and Conques. However, in the end I chose to begin in Vézelay, the assembly point for the Burgundians, mainly because I had long wanted to visit the famous Church of La Madeleine, also known as the church of the 'Men on the March' – a name to stir the blood of any traveller. Also, the south-westerly course from Vézelay appeared to promise the sort of rustic idyll that fitted my idea of pilgrimage, passing as it does over the many tributaries of the Loire, and through the valleys of the north-eastern edge of the Massif Central; with such towns as Charité sur Loire, Bourges, Perigeux, La Reòle and Bazas to add their spice of medieval architecture and history.

By the time I reached the foot of the Pyrenees, three of the routes would have come together, and the fourth, the one from Arles, would join soon afterwards at Puente la Reina – the Queen's Bridge. From that point to the shrine of St James, the four routes would be a single pathway striking westward across the varied landscape of northern Spain, through villages and towns that had been associated with the cult of St James for the last thousand years and more.

Having decided on my starting point, everything else fell neatly into place. Three weeks later, at the beginning of April – Chaucer's pilgrim season – I was waking up in Vézelay. Conveniently placed in the centre of France, in the rich lands of Burgundy, it was a site that had witnessed the making of much of Europe's history; here the Second Crusade was preached; at the steps of the high altar Richard Coeur de Lion had kept his vigil before setting out with his armies for the Holy Land; and from the tenth century onwards an endless river of pilgrims assembled here at the start of their long journey to Santiago de Compostela – St James of the Field of the Star. In a moving ceremony the pilgrims' small satchels, known as scrips, their staffs, their drinking gourds and their scallop shells – the symbols of St James – were blessed; and after making their confessions and taking communion, they donned their wind-resisting cloaks and their broad-brimmed hats – the front traditionally fastened back with a large scallop shell badge – and no doubt deeply affected by the stirring prayers of the 'Pilgrim's Itinerarium', they would stride off purposefully down 'The Way' towards distant Compostela, their feet not yet blistered nor frost-bitten, eager to cover the miles and to reap their eventual reward of a place in heaven.

And along with them would go the rogues, the cut-purses, the sellers of fake relics, women of easy virtue, acrobats, jugglers, troubadours, and the bevy of itinerant workers – stone masons, carpenters and others – who thronged the medieval roads of Europe trying to make a living by one means or another. The true pilgrim was further identified by his passport, which was both his official permission to make the journey and his guarantee of food and lodging at the monasteries along the route.

Although huge crowds still gather in Vézelay at Easter, Pentecost and on the feast day of St Mary Magdalene, two days after Easter the village was empty, and the only breakfast to be had was what we could put together ourselves with the aid of my small camping stove. We walked around the outside of the church, expecting it to be closed at that hour, but found a side door open, and so were able to visit it together before Peter had to leave on his long slow return to England with the Red Toad.

Apart from its vast size, the exterior of La Madeleine seen close to is not particularly impressive, but as on the previous evening, we found the first glimpse of its magnificent interior dazzling. Built at the height of medieval artistry with the unashamed intention of impressing, it more than succeeds. After the passage of nine centuries and with all the battering it sustained during the Wars of Religion, it is still overwhelming. It would have been worth a very long journey for the beauty and magnificence of the stone carvings alone, particularly the glorious narthex tympanum depicting the Risen Christ bestowing his power upon his apostles. Even the loss of one outstretched hand does little to rob this work of its extraordinary sense of presence. Many authorities consider it to be the most moving and profound of all the Romanesque carvings in Burgundy, and certainly it is one of the most poignant portrayals of Christ Enthroned that I have ever seen. Despite the triumphal nature of the subject, this is a Christ wholly involved in the world's suffering. The wonderfully carved face is full of sorrow, and the tremendous tension in the lines of the thin body and in the gesture of stretching out his elongated arms and hands beyond the disciples, as though to the whole creation, speak more of crucifixion than the joys of heaven. It seemed a strange and tragic anomaly that Christian knights should have ridden forth from such a doorway to slaughter infidels in the Holy Land in the name of this same gentle and sorrowing Christ.

But the great soaring edifice of Vézelay is also a shrine in its own right, built to house the relics of Mary Magdalene – a woman so unjustly dubbed 'fallen' by the early church on the flimsiest of New Testament evidence. Of course she would not have been half so interesting had she not been thought of as an adulteress; nor would her mortal remains have been half so valuable to Mother Church. But as a sinner, redeemed by Our Lord in person, she enjoyed star status. In the medieval world where even a splinter or two of bone from the ribs of a top-ranking saint were worth infinitely more than their weight in gold, and made the richest of gifts for a king, the worth of a complete corpse of such a mega-saint was incalculable.

Many of the objects of medieval veneration, such as phials containing drops of the Virgin's milk, Christ's blood, tears of holy martyrs, and so forth, were clearly spurious, and the wealth of fragments of the True Cross that abounded throughout Christendom would have furnished a small forest. In order to get hold of the whole or major part of a really important saint, however, shameful acts of theft were committed by clergy and laity alike, and even so, claims and counter claims were made about the whereabouts of innumerable relics, so the devout could often venerate the same saint in a choice of locations.

The relics of Mary Magdalene could certainly not be claimed to have arrived at Vézelay by altogether honest means. But the monk who was sent to get them from Aix justified his removal of the bones from their marble sarcophagus by the usual saint-inspired dream. It was generally accepted that a saint's relics had the power both to resist removal and to dictate the place of their final interment; keeping became, in a sense, proof of rightful ownership. Although Mary Magdalene's bones appeared to be happy to be translated to Vézelay, they refused to be carried into the monastery until the abbot and his monks had come out to greet her, and to sing Te Deum. After the formal installation it seems she had no desire to leave.

To the medieval mind, relics were not merely objects of veneration but possessed power in themselves, particularly powers of healing and intercession, which were commensurate with the saint's position in the heavenly hierarchy. Powers of healing were a particular draw in a world where diseases flourished, where the dreaded leprosy, plague and pestilence stalked the land, much as AIDS and cancer do nowadays. As modern man pins his hopes on science, so medieval man looked to miraculous intervention – though who would be so bold as to say that the two are entirely separate? Saints often became associated with particular cures, much as surgeons and doctors specialise today. Vézelay got off to a flying start with the story of a blind man who came to the shrine with the cry of 'If only I had eyes to see the shrine of the blessed Madeleine' and immediately regained his sight.

The intercession of saints on behalf of suppliants was of equal, if not greater importance. Life on earth being so very uncertain, and usually a good deal shorter, as well as considerably harder than it is today, the hereafter occupied people's thoughts a great deal more than it does now. Sin was taken seriously, for hell, with its hideous punishments loomed real and terrifying, and purgatory was little better. The loathsome creatures inhabiting both places, and the repulsive and hideous tortures perpetrated there were spawned in legion by the fertile imagination of the Middle Ages. Studying the horrific scenes, so plentifully depicted among the carvings on the walls and the capitals at Vézelay, I found it not surprising that people were eager to avoid eternal damnation.

Saints were thought of as inhabiting two places. They were present in their shrines certainly, but were also in the courts of heaven, where they were able to influence God on a penitent's behalf in much the same way as could a well-placed courtier who had the ear of his earthly king. And who better to intercede on a sinner's behalf than the woman who understood at first hand the frailty of human nature, and who had been among the first to see the Risen Lord? Perhaps it was the centuries of the prayers of pilgrims who felt they could identify with La Madeleine that gave

Vézelay its warm human quality in spite of its immense size. The anomaly is that scholarship has established, beyond all reasonable doubt, that the bones that were cherished here throughout all those centuries were almost certainly not those of Mary Magdalene at all.

It was in order to see more of the carvings, particularly the wonderfully lively capitals with their medieval beasts and purgatorial scenes that we climbed up to the gallery. After gazing our fill at all we could examine from there, we noticed a small door leading into the tower. This was a world apart from the glories of the church below, a place where the bones of the structure were revealed, and where massive frames of rough-hewn timber pinned the walls together. The wind howled through the embrasures as we climbed upwards, the stone steps giving way to flights of wooden slats, slippery with centuries of pigeon droppings. The higher we rose the more the building appeared to sway and rock in the wind, so that the analogy of a ship upon the waves was heightened. From the leads the view was enormous: together with the gargoyles we gazed down on a land struggling reluctantly into spring, earth showing bare in the fields, and black trees thrashing winter branches as they bent under the assaults of the wind. The year was not nearly so far advanced here as it had been in Southern England. It promised a tough beginning to my journey.

Retracing our steps after this excursion, we found the tower door locked and ourselves trapped on the stairs behind it. Whoever had turned the key had also gone far away, for although we shouted ourselves hoarse no one came. Churches on the Continent are often locked for days or weeks on end – the thought crossed my mind that we could moulder away in this windy tower until Pentecost. Patience might be a suitable virtue for pilgrims to cultivate, but immediate rescue was necessary if Peter was to get the unspeedy Toad to the ferry on time.

Studying the door, after a trial push or two had assured us that it would not yield, we wondered if the gap between the top of it and the stones of the sloping ceiling might not be just wide enough for a body to squeeze through. The only way to find out was to try, and since I was the smaller it made more sense for me to make the attempt. Before doubts could render me nervous I climbed onto a small projection from where I was able to push my feet and legs into the gap. With Peter's help I was then able to turn over so that I was facing downwards, and with my hands on his shoulders I could begin to push the rest of myself through. There was one horrid moment when my back was tight against the roof, legs dangling in space, and the thin top of the door cutting painfully into my solar plexus, making it difficult to breathe. I had either to retreat at once or commit myself to going forward. Fighting my fear of tight places, I squirmed and pushed until I stuck fast at chest level. Full of panic, but without the breath to call out, my compressed rib cage slowly changed shape, just sufficiently for wood and stone to relinquish their grip. Then all in a rush, like the final moments of birth, the rest of me slithered free, and I was on the other side of the door looking down on the vast interior spaces of the nave. A strange prelude to a journey I thought – though possibly escaping from incarceration, not to mention the symbolic rebirth, were not entirely inappropriate to the start of a pilgrimage.

A little while later, after Peter had been released by an apologetic workman who had gone off to breakfast with the key in his pocket, and without first checking that there was anyone in the tower, came the moment to say goodbye and depart in our separate directions. As a brisk cycle ride is an excellent way of taking the mind off the pain of parting, I did not go back into La Madeleine for another, more leisurely look as I had intended, but sped off down 'The Way', and was soon busy map-reading a course through the back lanes of Burgundy.

The abrupt departure felt somehow wrong. I had the vague sense of something missing, a feeling that there should have been some ceremony to mark my departure, or at the very least a blessing, to send me off properly prepared and in the right frame of mind. Excitement and anxiety are always present in roughly equal proportions when setting out, even on quite short undemanding jaunts, and although I hadn't as yet given much thought to the spiritual dimensions of this particular adventure, I was aware of embarking on no ordinary journey and felt inadequately launched. Since there was nothing I could do about it at that stage, however, I occupied my mind by going over my equipment, mentally checking the luggage, pannier by pannier as I rode, to make sure that I had left nothing behind. I was carrying rather a heavy load because in the interests of economy, and because I enjoy sleeping out, I planned to camp most nights. My small tent, sleeping bag, mattress, stove and pans, little pots of coffee and tea, candle, string, and all the odds and ends that go with simple camping weighed down the two large back panniers. Spare clothing, waterproofs, guide books, notebook and pens, something to read for pleasure, a very small radio and medicines filled the two smaller front panniers. Documents, money, penknife, an ultra-sonic sound device for seeing off ferocious dogs, and all other valuables went in the bag on the handlebars, and could easily be removed each time I left the bicycle. My tools, another weighty item, were kept separate to avoid getting dirt and oil on the other luggage, and I had just been given a very smart little bag for them which fitted neatly under the saddle. As soon as I thought about this toolbag I realised that something more mundane than prayer had been missing at the start of this journey. I stopped to check, and sure enough, the toolbag was not there. There was no possibility of the bag having fallen off; it must have been stolen.

There had been another bicycle alongside mine in the convent hall the previous evening, a tall, thin machine which belonged to a tall, thin Frenchwoman. She had arrived at the same time as us and had a scallop shell on her handlebar bag and a little plaque on her rear carrier which read *Chemin de St Jacques* – the Road of St James. But although she seemed clearly bound for the same destination as me, or else was returning from it, she had given only the curtest of nods in response to our greetings. Early as we had risen the following morning, she and her bike were already gone; and so, I now realised, was my toolbag. A cyclist's tool kit is a very precious and personal thing, assembled over many years, and with items highly customised for particular jobs: it wasn't just an attractive cycle accessory that was gone, but a well-tried friend. I wouldn't even be able to repair a puncture until I'd bought immediate and essential replacements. Annoying though it was, however, and hard thoughts though I certainly harboured against my fellow pilgrim (and as there was no one else in the convent except for the nuns, whom I could not suspect, I think she must have been the culprit), nonetheless, the incident gave quite an authentic medieval twist to the day, and in an odd way it supplied something of the connection with the past which I had felt was lacking. If there were still rogues preying on pilgrims on The Road to Compostela, who, or what, might I not meet as I travelled along it?

2

To be a Pilgrim

An implacable headwind, one of the worst conditions for cycling, made the going hard for the first few days. It was cold too, and altogether more like winter than early spring. Tall poplars lined the country roads, their bare branches hung with huge round balls of dark green mistletoe which added to the feeling of having strayed into an earlier season. Behind them the raw empty fields ran back to ancient, grey, sagging homesteads.

I had spent the previous six months finishing the manuscript of a book, and the long hours at my desk had not been good either for my cycling muscles or my general fitness. The older I get the more I realise the value of taking regular daily exercise, but as soon as I begin writing the task becomes so absorbing that there never seem to be sufficient hours in the day to get even the necessary things done, and my good resolutions are forgotten. Now I was paying the price, and even on Roberts, my excellent new bicycle, so well provided with low gears, I was finding it heavy going on the sharp little hills and was wondering if I was perhaps getting past the age for such vigorous physical exertions. To make matters worse a thin rain fell frequently, enough for me to have to ride in waterproofs. Modern wet weather clothing is supposed to 'breathe' and so prevent the rider becoming overheated, but I have never found any that stood up to this claim. Either the rain begins to seep through after an hour or two, or, if they are efficient at keeping the weather out they also make the rider sweat and become just as wet from condensation. Mine were definitely overheating.

Where my route sometimes left the lanes to follow more major roads, *camions* thundered closely alongside, tossing me about like a feather in the turbulence of their wake. Several times I was blown right off the tarmac, and only just managed to keep the bicycle upright and out of the ditch. In such conditions it made a break to reach a town and shop around for tools to replace my stolen set. Oddly enough in a country where the bicycle has always occupied a place of honour I wasn't able to find a single 'real' bicycle shop, but only modern motorcycle showrooms which included a small corner for the humbler machine. Everything in these smart emporia was expensively packaged, and the prices of perfectly ordinary spanners, tyre levers, allen keys and the like quite shocked me, so that I bought only the barest of necessities. It was as well that these included a puncture repair kit, because the following day I had a flat on a busy stretch of road, miles from anywhere.

I would not normally attempt to mend a puncture in the rain, but would simply fit a spare inner tube and do the repair at my leisure in the evening. Alas, both spare inners had been with my tools in the stolen bag; once again I experienced a strong unchristian twinge of animosity towards the thief, whoever it was. The puncture was small and difficult to find without a bowl of water in which to spot the tell-tale bubbles of escaping air. A rain puddle can serve for this purpose, but in spite of the continuing drizzle there were no useful pools when I needed them. Fortunately I had my small aluminium cooking pan and enough water in the drinking bottle to just cover the tube and so was eventually able to locate the hole. After that it was plain sailing, except for the difficulty of keeping the tube dry while I glued on the patch. I could not find what had caused the puncture, and this worried me: from past experience I knew there could be a thorn or a piece of sharp metal embedded in the tread of the tyre, so small as to be virtually invisible, and when the tyre is pumped up again, this hidden point will produce further punctures. A single thorn once caused me five separate punctures before I finally found it with the help of a strong magnifying glass. On this occasion, however, there was no further trouble, in fact it was to be the only puncture of the entire journey.

In spite of the generally inclement conditions, each day brought its crop of excitement and pleasure. There are always some good moments on a bicycle – moments when the spirits lift at the sight of a kestrel riding the wind, or when the clouds part and a shaft of wintry sunshine floods through to give a fleeting glimpse of forgotten glory; or when a rabbit or a hare, unaware of the bicycle's silent approach, is sitting up on its hind legs, twitching its whiskers and surveying the world. But most of the time if I thought about pilgrimage at all at this stage of my journey it was of the struggles of John Bunyan's Christian, rather than Chaucer's merry band.

> 'There's no discouragement
> Shall make him once relent
> His first avowed intent
> To be a pilgrim . . .'

Usually what kept me going was the anticipation of creature comforts – a good meal, a glass of wine, open fires, a hot bath, shelter from the unrelenting wind and rain, and the cessation of the daily struggle over the hard-won miles. And when I did reach the end of the day's ride I enjoyed these luxuries with all the relish that comes from having seemed to have won them by hard effort.

Camping in such weather was not an inviting prospect, and in any case, none of the official sites was as yet open; nor was it the sort of terrain for pitching the tent *au sauvage*. So for the first few nights I found economical accommodation like the Café de Paris, a pull-in for truckies at Charité sur Loire, where for 150 francs Roberts had a snug lock-up shed, and I was given a scrupulously clean linoleum-floored room furnished with three little white cots all in a row like a school dormitory, an ample dinner and my morning roll and coffee. Women were a great rarity in her establishment, the Madame told me, but it seemed I made a welcome change for she kept offering me extra little dishes to try, like her *fromage blanc* laced with shallots and black pepper, which was a speciality of the place.

Of Charité itself, once an important stopping place on the Road to Compostela where in 1059 the monks of Cluny built a famous monastery, I saw little beyond the venerable streets wet and gleaming and overwhelmed by modern traffic, and the swollen River Loire pounding through the stone arches of a sixteenth-century bridge. Tourism, the modern equivalent of pilgrimage, confines itself to more clement seasons, and so I found none of the churches or historic sites open, and could not even pay my respects to the famous statue of St James in the church of Sainte Croix.

What saved my journey in these early stages from

becoming just any long bicycle ride through France at the
wrong time of year was the need to get my pilgrim record
stamped. I had obtained this document in London, from
the Confraternity of St James, a society which had been
founded a few years earlier for the purpose of promoting the
pilgrim routes to Compostela. Several European countries
have created similar non-denominational societies in the
last decade in response to the sudden renewed interest in
the Santiago pilgrimage. There had been an abundance of
confraternities concerned with the cult of St James in the
later medieval period, particularly in France, with membership usually being confined to those who had successfully
made the pilgrimage. Members met regularly to worship
together, to perform good works and to advise and help
those wishing to make the pilgrimage to Compostela.

For me, membership of the Confraternity of St James
was a purely practical need at the outset of my journey,
giving me access to a small but useful library where I could
find out about the route and read up on the historical
background to the pilgrimage. I was also able to obtain
various guide books, including a translation of the part of
the twelfth-century *Codex Calixtinus* known as the 'Pilgrim's
Guide', a work written in about 1140 and usually attributed
to a French cleric named Aimery Picaud who came from
Pathenay-le-Vieux in Poitou. It was not a work to encourage
the faint-hearted for Picaud invariably found conditions
and people along the route extremely distasteful, if not
downright barbarous, especially when comparing either to
his native Poitou – a place he considered such a bastion of
civilisation in those uncertain times – that it was clearly
very brave of him to have left it, even for the purpose
of acquiring spiritual merit. I would join Picaud's route
south of Bordeaux, just before the crossing of the Pyrenees,

and I was looked forward to consulting his guide at the appropriate places.

From the Confraternity I had also been able to buy a silver scallop shell badge for my beret, and a bright red sweater emblazoned on the front with a small scallop shell, and on the back with a much larger one. These symbols would have to serve me as a modern equivalent of the St James pilgrim's garb, since cloak, broad-brimmed hat and staff, picturesque and practical though they might be for a walker, are certainly not suitable wear on a bicycle. The traditional Santiago costume, evolved from the practical need to protect a pilgrim from the extremes of sun, wind and rain, quickly became a uniform, and for sound reasons. Being immediately identifiable as a pilgrim conferred important benefits at a time when the roads were full of people on the move – artisans seeking work, people fleeing from plague and disease, and those whose livelihood was preying upon others. Strict laws existed in the Middle Ages for the protection of pilgrims, and harming or interfering with one was considered a very serious offence. Pilgrims were also exempted from paying tolls or local taxes, and, since the vast majority of them were poor (poverty being considered a Christian virtue in medieval times) they were also entitled to food, shelter and doctoring in the monasteries and hospices set up for that purpose along the route.

Since the roads of the twentieth century are equally thronged with traffic of a lethal nature, I hoped that the large shell on the back of my sweater would bring me benefits; in particular, that it would make truck drivers slow down and give me a wide berth when overtaking. But as wind and rain had as yet prevented me removing any outer layers I had not as yet been able to test modern sensitivity to the symbol of the pilgrimage. I also had a real scallop shell given me by my fishmonger, and this I had fastened to the front of my handlebar bag.

Why the scallop shell, since ancient times a symbol of the female, had been adopted as the badge of St James and his pilgrimage is explained by a fanciful legend, of which of course there are infinite variations. In fact, the entire saga of St James' association with Spain is so imaginative that coming to grips with it sheds considerable light on the world of the medieval pilgrim. The story goes that obeying Christ's instructions to preach the Gospel, St James drew Spain as his lot: the short straw it would seem, because after many weary years he had netted no more than a couple of converts. He returned to Jerusalem with these two disciples, and hard luck striking yet again, became the first of the apostles to be martyred; Herod ordering his execution by beheading. His two faithful disciples were told in a dream to take both head and body and make their way to the coast where a stone boat was waiting for them. Without oars or sail this boat made its way across the Mediterranean, passing between Scylla and Charybdis, ever westward, until it reached the coast of Spain and the very edge of the known world, coming finally to rest at the head of one of the long river inlets of Finisterre. A horse maddened by the sight of the stone boat, galloped into the ocean bearing its rider beneath the waves. When they emerged both were covered with large scallops, thereby setting the precedent for all later pilgrims to the shrine of St James.

A more mundane explanation for the adoption of the shell symbol, of course, is that like the palm leaves which Jerusalem pilgrims brought back from the Holy Land, the large scallop shells were a local feature and suitably distinctive. Unlike palms, or the crossed keys of the

Rome pilgrimage, scallop shells had the added advantage of making useful drinking vessels, handy for dipping into streams and rivers – their later employment as ashtrays was still a few hundred years off. At dinner one night it dawned on me that the delicious French dish called Coquille St Jacques was a uniquely Gallic way of honouring St James. By medieval times the motif of the scallop adorned churches, monasteries, fountains, wayside crosses, reliquaries and numerous other objects along the entire route. Even in countries as far flung as northern Britain and Poland there were numerous shell-hung St James' chapels showing how wide an appeal the pilgrimage enjoyed.

The 'Pilgrim's Record' which the Confraternity prepared for its members (and only those travelling by foot, horse or bicycle qualified as true pilgrims) had spaces for collecting the rubber-stamped symbols of significant churches along the route. With its pages duly filled, I could present this document on arrival at the shrine in Santiago, and if I satisfied the cathedral authorities that I had made the journey in a suitable spirit, I would be awarded my 'Compostela', the official certificate of the St James pilgrimage. This would not be the glittering prize for which my medieval forerunners risked their lives; for them, already blessed with the remissions of time spent in purgatory which they had been able to collect at important shrines along the way, arrival at Santiago meant a wiping out of one third of all their sins, and if the pilgrimage was made in a Jubilee or Holy Year, i.e. a year when the Saint's day fell on a Sunday, forgiveness was absolute (providing the pilgrim was also appropriately penitent). Medieval pilgrims also received their tangible record of completed pilgrimage, but as Compostelas did not bear the name of the recipient in their day, a brisk trade was to be made in them.

The immediate effect of collecting proof of my progress meant knocking on doors and making efforts with the French language. At Bourges, on my second day out, after wandering through the deathly cold, mouldering Gothic cathedral of St Etienne, vainly looking for a cleric with a rubber stamp, I was directed to the nearby presbytery, a building dating from much the same period, but warmer and infinitely more cheerful. Three priests, napkins tucked under chins were sitting at a well-stocked table in a room that without changing one detail could have been the film set for a period drama. They rose to welcome me, 'A pilgrim from England? Come in, come in. A Catholic? Ah well, no matter, Protestants are also welcome.' And in spite of my embarrassment at finding them at lunch (I tend to forget the lateness of provincial France's midday meal) and my attempts to escape, I was urged to seat myself and, at the very least, to take a glass of wine before the *tampon* was produced and my card stamped. '*Priez pour nous en Compostelle*,' they said as I departed half an hour later, as warmed by their friendliness as by the heavy local wine and rich pâté.

Issoudoun, Chateauroux, Neuvy St Sepulchre, Crozant, La Souterrain – slowly the pages began to fill with stamps, some with a handwritten tag underneath – '*Bonne Route*', '*Bon Voyage*', '*Bon Courage*', '*Paix et Joie*' and the lovely '*Priez pour nous*'. Seldom did I find a church actually open, nor did I meet another priest quite as hospitable as the three at Bourges, but those I did meet were friendly and approving, as though they considered I was doing a good thing, and one moreover in which they had a share. But pleasant though it always is to be thought well of, their respect made me a feel a little uncomfortable, as though I was inadvertently sailing under false colours. Although I

profess myself a Christian in the broadest sense of the term
– which is to say that while I am sure I would have been
excommunicated or burnt for my heretical views in an age
of strict orthodoxy, I managed to scrape together enough
tatters of faith and belief to see me through confirmation
in more flexible times. I certainly did not think of myself
as a pilgrim following a penitential path for the salvation
of my soul. As far as I was concerned I was making this
journey from the same motives as I made all my journeys,
in a spirit of enquiry and interest. After all, I enjoyed
travelling, and whereas I believed that all journeys were
a form of pilgrimage in the sense that they offered time and
space for reflection and for looking at life from a fresh angle,
I had no expectation of any particular reward or enhanced
spiritual state at the end of it. Since papal indulgences and
relics have long lost their credence for most of us, I couldn't
see that the route I was following was necessarily holier
than any other. It was the travelling that mattered. But
having people, and particularly priests, applaud my efforts
had the effect of making me think more closely about my
motivation in going to Santiago.

By the afternoon of the fourth day I decided I must make
an effort to camp. Hotels, even cheap ones, were eating
into my funds, and I also wanted more time in the quiet
and peace of my tent. All day I had been struggling across
a prairie-like countryside of factory farming, featureless
except for the occasional tattered stumps of blackthorn
that had defied the ruthless clearing process, and were not
only surviving, but valiantly sporting a few white blossoms.
There was nothing to break the force of the wind so that
by lunchtime it was an agony to push the pedals round.
I had just about reached the point of identifying with
the poor souls who had been sent off to Santiago as a

punishment for their wickedness, and whose chains and general air of despair had served as a horrid warning to other pilgrims when deliverance appeared in the shape of a Relais Routier.

Mellowed by boeuf bourgignon and a carafe of burgundy I was able to contemplate a further sixteen miles to Neuvy St Sepulchre. Above me dark clouds had gathered in towering columns, ranged like opposing forces in an antique war of the gods. Beneath them the scenery had changed into real countryside again, with steep little fields, and sheep, lambs and cattle safe behind thick hedgerows. A sudden swift downpour of rattling hailstones ceased just as abruptly to reveal expanses of clear blue across which the massed clouds galloped, their enormous shadows racing before them over the undulating ground – all wonderful lighting effects for the ruined tower and church which now hove into view at the top of a small hill. This was the one-time stronghold of the Ducs of Cluis Dessous, and as I walked about the grassed-over mounds that had been the curtain wall, the wind dropped and the sun grew hot. And it was all so delightful looking out over the wide landscape that I would have thrown up my little tent there and then, and settled down to enjoy it all, had not an old proprietorial gentleman come over to chat with me and to tell me that I should ride on to Cluis and ask at the *Mairie* – the town hall – for a place to camp.

My elation with what seemed to be the return of spring carried me on the few miles to Cluis, a sleepy little village with a brand new *Mairie* and plans for opening a camping site to encourage tourism. It would all be ready in another year or two explained the two ladies in charge (when they could recover sufficiently from the fit of giggling brought on by my abuse of their language). The fluency of my

French had recently been greatly improved by several months spent travelling through French West Africa to Timbuktu. But as the colonial version of their tongue sounds quite barbarous to French ears, my use of it caused a good deal of amusement. Fortunately, an ex-schoolmaster, Robert Rigaud, was also visiting the *Mairie*, and he came to the rescue with an impressive command of English. When he had grasped that what I was looking for was a spot of ground to pitch my tent on, he invited me to come home with him and see if his garden would suit. Several hours later, after drinking quantities of tea with Robert and his wife Jeanne, and chatting about England, where they spent all their holidays, there was no question of me sleeping in my tent. The Rigauds had lots of spare room and anyway, staying with them was not unlike camping, comfortable though I was made. Robert had been preparing the house for their retirement for about a dozen years, he told me, doing most of the work himself, and to a very high standard, but because he was involved in so many other activities, both civic and private, it was never likely to be completely finished. Moreover, since he retired, he had discovered one over-riding passion which was threatening to leave him no time for anything else at all. This was the garden around the house, a garden he was creating from the wilderness, and which he had already planted so closely with trees, shrubs and vegetables that I doubt there would have been room in it even for my small tent. But in spite of its unfinished state the house breathed such an air of peace that I slept more deeply there than I had in a long while.

I left the friendly Rigauds in weather that continued delightfully sunny, so I dared to hope that spring was now here to stay, and rode on through pretty hilly countryside on the western fringes of the Massif Central that was slashed by deep river beds. For once there was almost no wind, and in the stillness I heard my first cuckoo of the year. Lunch was bread and cheese *sur l'herbe* on a high ridge watching a pair of buzzards lazily practising aerobatics while I boiled a second kettle for coffee – the first having overturned because of my preoccupation with these most marvellous of aerial performers. This was more what I had imagined the journey would be like – an idyllic springtime passage through a pleasant land. And so it continued for a few days, days of soft sunshine full of the fresh scents of growing things and the calls of woodpeckers and cuckoos, small hawks and buzzards.

Night stops were not always quite so Arcadian. Because of the paucity of camping sites I had to stay in places I would not normally choose. Once, at the say so of a resident, I pitched the tent beside a stream on the outskirts of a village, and was much plagued by an elderly bibulous gentleman who seemed to think I might succumb to his Gallic charm if he was persistent enough. Even when I succeeded in repulsing him, he remained in close proximity, and whenever I looked up from my book, his large purple nose was pointed in my direction, with his bloodshot eyes wearing the reproachful expression of a rejected hound. He retired to the village bar just before nightfall where presumably he soon became *hors de combat* for he gave me no further trouble.

At Perigueux I camped on the banks of the Isle, a fine impetuous river rippling over falls and weirs with the town perched high above it on the northern bank. Here, according to my Aimery Picaud guide, I should be venerating the relics of St Front, a very holy bishop consecrated by St Peter himself, and with numerous miracles to his credit. Probably the church would have been locked anyway, like most of the others, but I forgot all about St Front in my search for a square meal. By this stage of the journey, with all the fresh air and exercise, my appetite was prodigious, and Perigueux seemed not over-supplied with restaurants. I found an ancient hotel eventually, dark brown in colour, and in atmosphere a little like Dracula's castle. I was the only guest in the cavernous, dimly lit dining room, where a large-bosomed brassy-haired Madame sat in state at a raised mahogany cash desk near the entrance, watching over the creepy waiter who, bent like a hairpin, brought me course after course. Every now and then a distracted-looking chef put his head around the corner and made frantic signs which were ignored by the other two. He was supposed to be guarding my bicycle in his kitchen, as Madame had decided that Perigueux was not a safe place to leave even a locked bicycle outside. Though adequate, I cannot claim it was a gastronomically memorable meal, but it certainly had high entertainment value – and for all concerned. For when I went to collect *Robert* as the bicycle tended to be called in France because of the name of the maker inscribed on the downtube – the second syllable lengthened lovingly, making it a much nicer sounding name I thought than plain English Roberts – I found that the chef and his large fierce-looking assistant were having a high old time riding *Robert* around the kitchen.

Going back along the river bank was lovely. A thin mist was rising from the water, and everything seemed so romantic and eighteenth century in the soft moonlight, a total contrast with the previous raw evening which I had spent on a municipal site between St Leonard de Noblat and Limoges. St Leonard's relics were also worth a mega-star according to Aimery Picaud, but I had missed this saint too and any possible indulgences I might have earned, mainly because Picaud got so involved and heated in his writing about different towns laying claim to the possession of the same St Leonard that I was no longer sure where I should venerate this champion of prisoners whose shrine was supposed to be so atmospherically hung about with chains brought there by grateful freed captives. Also the route from Vézelay was not proving very easy to follow, mainly because of the numerous possible variations, so even had I been heading in the right direction I might still have missed St Leonard.

The municipal site was rather a bleak spot on a hill beside a rough sloping football field, and plagued by some full-time travellers whom, I understand, are more plentiful in France than in Britain and have become quite a problem. The local councils try to keep them out of the general camp sites as they have a depressing effect upon tourism. Coming into contact with just a few of them gave me some sympathy for the authorities, though there is the question of providing adequate facilities for the travellers, which is not being met. Certainly these people didn't fit into the usual civilised French camping scene. Free-ranging lurcher dogs and tough children beating up the place on high-revving miniature motor bikes most effectively shattered the peace. The women had completely taken over the toilet block to do their mountain of washing, while their sinister-looking men took turns to patrol endlessly up and down within yards of my tent, staring boldly and fixedly at me each time they came level. Having such a small and adaptable tent, I can pitch it almost anywhere, and on this occasion I had chosen a spot under the peripheral belt of trees so as to be as far away as possible from the noise and commotion, so the prowling men had to go out of their way to pass so closely. I didn't think their behaviour was anything more

29

threatening than the unfocused hostility of a minority group whose life-style attracted so much official harassment, but it made me nervous, and I didn't feel I could leave the tent or the bicycle unguarded.

It turned very cold in the night, and I hadn't the energy to crawl out and pile on more clothing, but burrowed down more deeply into the sleeping bag instead, warming myself with my own breathing. I slept quite well in spite of the travellers, because before I'd turned in I had made the acquaintance of a German couple, Ilse and Dirk, who were also using the site that night and whose caravan was parked not far away, so I did not feel so completely isolated among strangers as I had earlier. I had met them passing to and fro from the shower block, and we had exchanged the usual pleasantries, commenting on the weather and the paucity of camping sites. Later they had invited me into their smart, neat caravan for coffee, and then pressed me to stay for a meal.

It was obvious that there was something physically very wrong with Dirk, he looked so ill and frail, and I must have said something or asked a question that invited confidence, or we might not otherwise have progressed beyond safe conversational topics. They appeared to be very self-contained people, but having begun, the relief of talking openly, especially with a stranger, overcame barriers, and they told me that Dirk was suffering from a virulent form of osteoporosis and had not long to live. The illness had been brought on by drugs prescribed, he said, for a completely different and far less serious condition, and he had been fighting the effects for a year or so, during which time his stature had been shrinking dramatically. He was determined now to use what time he had left to the full, which was why they were making this trip through the

French countryside which he and Ilse had always loved. They couldn't wait for warmer weather, because already Dirk was finding it very tiring to drive far, or indeed to move about much at all, and they had been forced to exchange their more manoeuvrable motor home for a caravan in order to provide greater comfort for him. I could see he was not the sort of man who would give up any activity without a struggle, and that poor Ilse would have to watch and be unable to intervene or help in any way until he allowed her to, and I thought the ordeal they were living through was probably far more heart-breaking for her than for Dirk himself.

I learnt that he was a highly successful man financially, and owned an international computer concern which he ran with his son. But since his illness his ideas had altered and his priorities had changed, he said. Now he wished his son would explore life a little more while he was still young, and think of money and responsibilities a little less. I asked him jokingly if he would prefer a son like mine, who was much the same age as his, but who was a confirmed wanderer, a young man who spent his life sailing the seas single-handed, owning nothing other than the small boat he lived in, and working only when he needed to top up his bank balance. I expected him to reply in the same vein, with something like 'perhaps an amalgam of the two young men might be a good thing'. Instead, Dirk said solemnly that I should be happy to have raised such a child, at which I had to confess that whatever the world thought about it, I found very little to complain of in the way my son had chosen to live his life. 'I should think not indeed,' laughed Ilse. 'What sort of example does his mother set him?' And suddenly all three of us were laughing, gratefully, spinning it out, because humour was so wonderfully refreshing after all this dark serious talk of death. They had wanted to ask me in, confided Ilse before I left them, because with my bicycle and the dumpy little tent I summed up for Dirk the sense of freedom that sometimes pierced him like a knife when he remembered the long summers of his youth, riding or hiking through the German countryside with the whole of his life still before him.

I asked them where they would be heading for after this, but they said they didn't know, they just wanted to keep on moving as long as possible. They had reached the stage where they could no longer anticipate anything, even the next day, with any great certainty, but had to live each moment as it came – which, as I suddenly remembered, is what many religious disciplines consider to be the only way to live. Not that Ilse and Dirk had professed any religion; they were simply on a journey, as I was. Our paths had crossed, we had told each other our stories, and were ready to go our separate ways. When I struck camp the following morning, breakfasting on a cup of coffee and a slightly wrinkled orange, which was all I had left, their van was still shuttered and silent, so there were no farewells, but I thought about them often in the next few days, and although they hadn't asked it of me, I added them to the growing list of those to pray for in Compostela.

3

Soft Southern Lands

The intimate countryside of the Bergerac wines made me realise afresh just how lucky I was to have discovered the bicycle as a means of long-distance travel. The close little valleys with their winding narrow roads and vine-clad hills crowned with modest stone chateaux, all of which could be seen to perfection at ten miles an hour, were far too tortuous and on far too small a scale to be enjoyed by motor car. The whole area was a little world apart, and would have been missed altogether on anything like a proper road. But with the sun shining, the pedals spinning round with just enough effort to match my energy, and no motorised traffic to mask the scents of the countryside or to drown the birdsong, I felt a sense of peace with myself and with the world about me that I rarely achieve in the frenetic bustle of modern life.

A short stretch of tree-shaded back lanes brought me at length down to the River Garonne at La Réole, a charming small town, slightly rackety and run down at one end, but graced with streets of well-preserved medieval houses at the other. A very large and ornate seventeenth-century Benedictine abbey at the centre of the old quarter had been converted into the *Hôtel de Ville*, lending the sleepy place

a rather lop-sided air of importance, as though recalling its
days of grandeur when the English kings, through marriage
and inheritance, owned practically as much land in France
as did the French crown; when this town had been at the
hub of things, and had played host to Richard Coeur de
Lion and later to Edward the Black Prince.

It played host to me too in a small grassy *campement* beside
the broad, brown Garonne, which looked particularly welcoming to a tired traveller in the late afternoon sun. The site
was officially closed, but the concierge said she would turn a
blind eye to a one-night stopover, as long as I did not make
myself conspicuous. With the site plainly visible from the
town, and the river front open to all, including half a dozen
patient fishermen who seemed to be permanent fixtures,
I didn't quite see how my presence could go unnoticed.
Also, finding hot and cold water conveniently to hand in
the as yet unfinished sani block, I could not resist a general
rinsing out of sweaty clothing, which had then to be strung
out to dry on the guy lines, where they considerably raised
the profile of my discreet, low, green tent.

I compromised by removing myself from the scene,
and with that virtuous feeling that comes from having
completed even such minimum and prosaic chores, left the
place to the anglers and crossed back over the suspension
bridge into La Réole in search of a stamp for my pilgrim
record and an evening meal. Neither proved easy. I hadn't
found an open church in days, and was beginning to wonder
if France had turned its back on Christianity altogether.
The plump *curé* whom I eventually tracked down was
anything but welcoming, and only grudgingly unlocked
the impressive Benedictine church for me to take a quick
look while he searched for his rubber stamp. Having found
it, he applied it to my card with such haughty carelessness

that the blue cameo image of a haloed figure was only an indistinct blur, and the name La Réole had to be written in by hand. There was no friendly addition of a 'Bon Voyage' or 'Priez pour nous'.

The only food I managed to find was a pizza, which proved as expensive as a more typically French provincial meal would have been, and far less satisfying. It seemed strange that a fast-food café could flourish in a country so gastronomically gifted; but since every table was taken, I was clearly in the minority with my preferences.

It occurred to me as I sat there sipping my coffee (which at least was typically French) that for someone who was following a pilgrimage, I was perhaps giving altogether too much thought to food and comfort. Was this, I wondered, because of the absence of open churches to provide a different focus for my travels? It must surely have been easier to keep the mind on more spiritual matters in earlier ages, with a daily mass, the possibility of hearing any or all of the six monastic offices, as well as the presence of other pilgrims? Because Latin was used in church services throughout Western Christendom, it provided pilgrims with their most familiar reference point among all the foreign tongues and strange customs they encountered along the way.

But then religion and spirituality are not necessarily the same. Maybe the very abundance of religious observance produced a kind of mental inertia, or a weariness of spirit that, together with the selling of indulgences and other abuses of the Catholic Church, would eventually lead to the 'Protest' and the Protestant faith. And necessary though it surely was to end the scandals and rekindle a less worldly spirit in the Church, the trouble with the Protestant split was that it went on protesting and splitting off into ever more separate churches and sects, as it is still doing to this very day in America. The glory of the single indivisible Church of Christ might still be a religious concept, but it is no longer a tangible reality as it was for the medieval pilgrim.

Where the medieval pilgrim knew only one immutable faith with which he could walk in security, the modern pilgrim is aware of half a dozen great world religions, as well as their endless shades of meaning and problems of interpretation. Monasteries had been non-existent on my trail, and the only church I had entered in the past few days, apart from the few moments in the huge vaulted expanse at La Réole, was a small apsed chapel in the middle of nowhere, a lonely neglected little building, furnished with a font shaped like a mortar and suitably decorated with scallop shells. Far more rivetting than the emblem of St James, however, had been the filigree curtain of spider webs behind the altar. Alight in golden sunshine streaming through the narrow lancet windows, it had made nature seem infinitely more attractive than mouldering stone. Could it be that this pilgrimage was turning me into a pagan, a mere worshipper of nature?

Mulling over these thoughts in La Réole's brash plastic pizza house, while in the square outside couples strolled casually about in that lovely hour at the end of the day when time itself seems to have slowed down and taken on a more mellow pace, I remembered that in St Luke's Gospel, where the story of the road to Emmaus is told, it was at this same hour, when they were sitting down to eat, that two disciples of Jesus had recognised their Risen Lord in the stranger at table with them. He had been walking and talking with them all day, comforting them in their distress about the Crucifixion, but it was only in the simple act of the breaking of the bread that they saw him for who he truly was. And the moment they recognised him, he vanished.

I remembered too that most of my best moments so far on this trip had had nothing to do with churches, but had been at times like this, when relaxed and expecting nothing I had suddenly become aware of a wider reality than my own narrow concerns. There was nothing in these experiences that I could put a name to, no revelation like seeing the Risen Christ, or arriving at the solution to some profound problem, just a sense of joy, too intense to last more than a moment, but leaving behind it a warm feeling of comfort, like the words of that great medieval Christian mystic, Dame Julian of Norwich: 'And all will be well, and all manner of things will be well.'

Back at my camp site the anglers appeared not to have moved since I left – models of contentment. They fished on as the daylight dimmed and electric lights sprang out of the gathering dark. Across the river an occasional train trundled its way westward to Bordeaux or eastward to Toulouse, giving a melancholy wail as it passed through the small station. I wrote up my journal, straining to see in the last of the light, reluctant to leave the world of the river and retire into the tent behind the mosquito netting, where I could use the torch without being inundated with flying insects.

Now I could no longer see it, I was more actively aware of the low continuous roaring of the river. I found it a soothing sound, reassuring, like the audible breathing of a trusty companion. Long since tamed; safely confined between solid banks and plentifully provided with convenient bridges, it isn't easy to imagine the rivers of Europe as T.S. Eliot's 'strong brown gods – sullen, intractable, destroying'. Only after four months' journey along the largely unconquered River Niger in West Africa did I gain some degree of understanding about the geographical hazards faced by medieval travellers in regions lacking both roads and bridges. When the barrier was as wide and powerful as the Garonne the prospect was formidable indeed, but getting across any unbridged river was one of the major hazards of medieval pilgrimage, as Aimery Picaud's account of a ferry crossing in Gascony so graphically describes:

'Their boat is small, made from a single tree trunk, ill-suited to carry horses; and so when you get into the boat you must take care not to fall into the water. You will do well to hold on to your horse's bridle and let it swim behind the boat. Nor should you get into a boat that has too many passengers, for if it is overloaded it will at once capsize.

Often, too, having taken the passengers' money, the boatmen take such a number of passengers on board that the boat overturns and the pilgrims are drowned; and then the wicked boatmen are delighted and appropriate the possessions of the dead.'

That night a short sketch featured in my dreams:

A poor thirteenth-century pilgrim enters La Réole. Asks a fat priest (looking very like the one I had encountered) for a seal upon his pilgrim's passport. Fat priest is arrogant and dismissive.

Enter Richard Coeur de Lion clad in full Crusader armour. He has overheard the exchange and berates the fat priest for his lack of Christian charity. As a penance (much to the embarrassment of the pilgrim and the fury of the priest), Richard orders the priest to wash the pilgrim's feet.

Which was possibly the result of all my thoughts and experiences of the day being woven into shape by sleeping so near to swift running water.

I was on my way by eight the following day having first cooked a most beautiful fried egg (quite a triumph in a thin aluminium pan). The tent was still wet with dew, but I couldn't wait for it to dry. The ancient pilgrim map I had with me marked the Garonne as a major dividing line, and having crossed it, I felt I had reached a significant point in the journey and was impatient to press on.

Thinking about rivers, and about how fortunate I was to be able to cross them under my own steam without being at the mercy of villainous ferrymen and the like, occupied the short distance to Bazas, so that I noticed little about the route except that it was pleasant and rural.

Bazas jerked me into the present. Calm and golden in the early morning sunshine, it looked the sort of provincial town where nothing more exciting than the weekly market ever happens. But it was in fact a town where one of the most decisive events in medieval history had taken place; the town where the Church Militant had its official beginnings. Here in 1095, Pope Urban II preached the First Crusade – a holy war, no less, against the forces of Islam which were barring the way to Jerusalem. It was a call that sent a tidal wave of change crashing through the Western and Near-Eastern worlds, the ripples of which spread out as far as Mongolia, and could be said to be still active nine hundred years later in territories like the former Yugoslavia. It was also an extraordinary doctrinal departure in the name of a religion that stood primarily for peace and which preached the virtues of loving one's enemies and of turning the other cheek. True, the Emperor Constantine had changed Christianity for ever when he had adopted it as the state religion more than seven hundred years earlier. But it could be argued that while he had fought under the banner of Christianity (although no Christian himself), it had been in order to defend his rightful territories, to secure the peace of his empire. A 'Holy War' to conquer fresh territory was, strictly speaking, a Muslim concept – *Jihad* – the natural expression of a religion which believed with a burning conviction that it was 'Better dead than not a Muslim' and sought to impose Islam wherever human life existed.

Within little more than a hundred years of the Prophet Mohammed's death, the unquenchable religious zeal of Islam had won, in the name of Allah, a vast empire, stretching from the Bedouin Arabian homelands, right through the Levant, across North Africa and taking in all of Spain, except for a narrow strip along the northern coast. Nor had it stopped at the Pyrenees. Very soon Muslim forces were ransacking French towns like Autun and Narbonne, laying seige to Toulouse and marching on towards Paris and the English Channel. All of Europe was potentially under threat. It was the nightmare of the eighth century, and a dread that was to continue unabated for several hundred years. As the historian Edward Gibbon was to write of the period, it really was touch and go that Britain along with Europe did not become part of the great Islamic Empire. And it is against the background of that dread that the age has to be seen. Islam was effectively the 'Anti-Christ'.

The first great headlong onslaught of Islam had been halted three hundred and fifty years before Urban II made his impassioned call to arms at Bazas. According to Gibbon the one man responsible for preserving Europe, and by extension Britain, for Christianity was Charles Martel, grandfather of the more famous Charlemagne, and founder of the Carolingian dynasty in France. Charles Martel subjected the Muslims to their first defeat in pitched battle at Poitiers in 732 AD. More importantly, perhaps, he was able to establish an efficient feudal system in his realms, enabling him to raise and maintain an army that could be an effective counter to the continuing Islamic threat. Muslim forces continued to cross the Pyrenees during the next hundred years, sometimes pushing deeply into French lands, but on each occasion they were defeated.

In Spain, however, the Moorish culture became firmly established, flourishing in all branches of learning and the arts. Indeed, so great was the flowering that for a short time, during the Caliphate of Cordoba, Spain rather than Baghdad was the centre of the Islamic world, and the thin strip of Christian-held land along the northern edge of the peninsular was under constant threat of invasion, particularly after Santiago de Compostela became a focus for Christian pilgrimage.

It was in 814 AD, at a point towards the western end of that Christian-held, sea-bordered strip, that a monk named Pelayo had a vision which was to prove so far reaching in its effect as to reverse the tide of Islamic conquest in Spain. Pelayo dreamt that a star would lead him to a field where the body of St James the Great, son of Zebedee, brother of John, and one of the principal disciples of Jesus lay buried. He told his local bishop of his vision; the spot was excavated and a sarcophagus containing three sets of bones was unearthed. These were triumphantly hailed as the remains of St James and his two disciples, a claim which was almost immediately endorsed by the Pope. St James was proclaimed patron saint of Spain, a church was built over the site, and what must have been the most convenient discovery ever of a major relic launched one of the world's major pilgrimages. It was also to be of prime importance in the 'Reconquest' of Spain.

As had long been noted, the great force and power of Islam came from the religious fanaticism of its warriors. Pilgrimage to Mecca, which was the goal of every pious Muslim, added to death in battle against the infidel, brought instant translation to Paradise. Christianity desperately needed something to counter such military zeal. It came in 844, at the Battle of Clavijo, in the Rioja. Thirty years after the discovery of the tomb of St James, the patron saint was seen clad in shining armour, mounted on a white charger at the head of the Christian army, holding aloft a white banner emblazoned with a blood-red cross. In his right hand he gripped a great sword, and the severed Muslim heads were falling before his onslaught like grain in a wheat field. And though there was never any mention of the Battle of Clavijo until the end of the twelfth century, by that time St James was long established in his dual role, and was depicted accordingly in statues and illustrations. He was *Santiago Peregrino*, the gentle and archetypal pilgrim to his own shrine, and also *Santiago Matamoros* – St James the Slayer of Moors, defender of his shrine and of all those who journeyed there. Islam was no longer the only side with the zeal of religious conviction. God, or at least his 'Saint of Battle' was fighting on the side of the Christians.

Nonetheless, the St James pilgrimage must have been a real journey of courage in those early days, with the ever-present threat of death or capture by the Moors to add to the other perils and hardships. Even a century and a half after the debatable Battle of Clavijo, the shrine itself was not safe from attack. In 997, the little town of Santiago which had grown up around the Field of the Star, was sacked by the war lord Al-Mansur and the bells of the church were removed to Cordoba.

The idea of militant Christianity had taken a permanent hold, however, and nothing was going to shift it now. *Deus Vult* – God wills it, preached Urban II in this forgotten little town of Bazas, urging all able-bodied men in Christendom to carry the battle into Muslim lands. At the time it might well have seemed that God did indeed will it. For by 1095 much had changed in the balance of power between Muslim and Christian. In Spain the Reconquest was well under way, and Christianity had gained an entirely new image; one learnt, it would seem, from its greatest rival. The wonder is that in between all this fighting for territorial control, the Gospel of Peace preached by Jesus of Nazareth survived at all.

In front of Bazas's cathedral which, like the square in which it stands, is enormous for the size of the town, I met a despondent American. 'Don't they ever open their churches around here?' he asked. 'Seems tourism doesn't count for much with the French.' I could only offer heartfelt sympathy, and add that pilgrimage didn't count for much either. Later I discovered the presbytery, had my record stamped, and gained admittance to the interior of the church; by which time the American had departed in disgust. Had I met him again I could have told him he had already seen the best, for the interior was nothing compared with the west front, before which we had voiced our complaints.

This architectural gem is all that is left of the medieval church. Like everything around these parts, it suffered badly in the Wars of Religion, but nonetheless, this fragment is still magnificent if only for its amazing sense of antiquity. It is like a great stone triptych, with three evenly spaced doors, and above each a superb tympanum heavily encrusted with carvings, one to the Virgin, one to St Peter and one of the Last Judgement. Like so much medieval carving it possesses a deeply devotional quality, like a call to prayer. I thought of Urban II, the head of the Christian Church, with his back to this great statement of faith, preaching death and destruction to the Muslim infidels – a message so at odds with the work behind him.

Thinking of the events that had begun at Bazas was to realise how the Church, with the Pope at its head, was right at the forefront of world power at this time. Nor was it difficult to see the purely practical, some might even say cynical, reasons for the Church to promote the Santiago pilgrimage. What was less easy to understand was how the pilgrims themselves fitted into this highly political scene, motivated as most of them must have been at this time by true piety and devotion. It would take another two hundred years and the establishment of comfortable inns along the way for Chaucer's more tourist-minded pilgrims to emerge. And anyway, the type of pilgrim who was attracted by the holiday aspect of pilgrimage tended to go on the shorter journeys to local shrines like Canterbury or Walsingham, which did not carry anything like the same risks or hardships. A pilgrim had to be very determined indeed to set his sights on Santiago. So what, I wondered, did eleventh-century pilgrims make of one of Jesus's disciples becoming the bloodthirsty *Santiago Matamoros* 'Slayer of Moors'? A disciple, moreover, who had been present at all the most important of the Gospel events, like the Transfiguration and the Agony in the Garden?

Soon after Bazas I descended to the flat sandy plains of Les Landes, where I really had no choice but to ride on the D 932 which was a main road. But for once the wind was behind me so that I fairly sped down the long straight stretches of tarmac that run through acres of dark forests. The golden day became hotter and hotter and in each small clearing I passed there were couples and families eating a leisurely lunch at wooden picnic tables. This meant fewer vehicles on the busy road and I decided to take full advantage of the lull. In any case the easy exhilarating riding made me forget hunger and thirst and I did all of the thirty miles to Roquefort in one glorious spurt.

Roquefort is not where the famous cheese comes from, I discovered to my disappointment: it was made in other villages in the area and had got its name from being marketed in Roquefort. The town's importance is that it is the only place for many miles where a wide tributary of the River Douze can be crossed. As a consequence of this, several roads converged on the bottle neck of the narrow bridge, and it was the point at which the day's euphoria ceased in the racket and fumes of long lines of lorries. The pavement was the only relatively safe place for a bicycle, and as I walked along it, I realised that the saying about it being too noisy to hear oneself think is literally true.

Under the circumstances it was a relief to learn that Roquefort's camping was 'broken' and to be directed to Sarbazan, a small village two kilometres away, where my tent soon stood in solitary state among glades of tall pines.

Picaud describes the area of Les Landes as 'desolate country', lacking in everything: 'there is neither bread nor wine nor meat nor fish nor water nor any springs' he warns. Things have changed. I had a particularly sumptuous dinner of many kinds of smoked meats, an excellent salmon pasta dish and a good steak, all of which I could only do adequate justice to because of having foregone lunch. So

45

good was the food, and so abundant that the meal went on much longer than usual. Even the *crème caramel* was twice the usual size. By the time I had paid the bill it was pitch black and a full-scale thunderstorm was in progress.

I had a mile or so of woodland tracks to negotiate to get back to my camp, and all I possessed in the way of lights was a mini caving lamp which fitted on the front of my head by means of an elastic harness. This was excellent for reading or writing in the tent; it also made a useful emergency front lamp when riding – at least it enabled oncoming traffic to see me; but it did little to illuminate the rough, root-encumbered ground.

'Thank you God and all the blessed saints and angels who look after foolhardy travellers,' began that night's entry in the journal. For somehow I was guided back to the small, hump-backed, fragile bit of nylon which was my temporary home in that black, sodden world. And how that could have been achieved without braining myself on a tree or mangling Roberts among the many hazards was a feat I could only put down to Divine Intervention.

Having accomplished the difficult task of getting myself inside the tiny low tent without soaking everything in it; and now warm and dry in my sleeping bag and dutifully writing up my notes, the rumbling thunder and the tumultuous rain only added to the feeling of safety laced with the spice of adventure.

4

Towards the Pyrenees

The countryside changed again as I crossed the River Adour and found the road rising sharply in front of me. Gone in the instant were the broad flat plains of Les Landes with their scents of resinous pine forests and sandy heathlands. On either side now were hills rolling on southwards towards the high Pyrenees, and there was a cool fresh hint of mountain air.

By the time I had adjusted to the increased demands of the terrain and settled my pedalling rhythm to the right gear, I had arrived at the small town of St Sever and was happy to turn off the road and think about lunch. St Sever was an unexpected delight; as medieval a town as any twentieth-century pilgrim could hope for, built in the round with a particularly lovely Romanesque church at its centre. And perhaps because it was market day, this church was not only open, but its dark interior was warm and welcoming with islands of soft candlelight. Men and women came one by one out of the shadows with the matter-of-fact air of long custom. As they stood before the pricket lighting their candles and murmuring a brief prayer, their heads were haloed in the warm yellow light, and took on the drama and beauty of a Rembrandt painting.

I felt at home there, for lighting candles as a focus for prayer is one of the many customs that makes me glad to be a part of the High Anglican tradition, rather than the broad or the low. Some Christians need such drama – 'the smells and bells' – as it is often slightingly described by those who prefer a plain, no-nonsense approach. I remember an old lady defending her High Church practices to a young visiting cleric of strong evangelical persuasion who had referred disparagingly in his sermon to 'mere musical Christians', implying that High Anglicans are more interested in the beautiful external trappings of their faith than in the hard core of the Christian message; that they confuse church with theatre. 'Young man,' she said, 'there is a lot of very indifferent drama enacted at the theatre and the opera, but people pay good money to go to it, so they must get something from it. The life and death of Jesus Christ is the most dramatic and moving story ever written, so why on earth should we not celebrate it with all the beauty, skill and passion at our command?'

Candles are particularly important because the celebration of light and heat as the great gifts of God is something that we share, not only with Roman Catholics and the Greek and Russian Orthodox Churches, but also with Buddhists, Hindus, Jews and people of many other faiths. And it was through this same ritual that I first gained an insight into the strong core of unity that exists within the wide diversity of beliefs. It was when I was making a journey through the Himalayas and had come to a Tantric Buddhist temple in a remote part of Sikkim. An elaborate exorcism ceremony was in progress in the vast hall, and every gesture and sound of the colourful, involved ritual were alien to me, and even somewhat repellant at first.

Yet at the same time I had this sense of recognition, of being in some way connected with it. Eventually I realised that this was because of the worshippers drifting around the perimeter of the hall in ones and twos to light yet another of the hundreds of reeking little butter lamps, adding their visible token to the universal prayer.

Since the dawn of man's existence on the planet, fire has inspired him with feelings of awe and wonder – emotions that lie at the very heart of the religious response. To the Ancient Greeks fire was a gift so precious that it had to be stolen from the Olympian gods and paid for by the torments of Prometheus. The Christian Church made it central to its drama and liturgy from the very beginning – in the Descent of Holy Fire at Easter, in the Light of Christ, and in the Flames of Pentecost, when it signals the descent of the Holy Spirit and is accompanied by the great 'gift of tongues'.

And here was I in the twentieth century, seated in an ancient church in a small town, feeling that I was a part of this long celebration of light and fire as I read through the medieval prayers in my sadly neglected 'Pilgrim's Itinerarium'. I had fully intended going through these prayers each day to put me in the proper state of mind for the journey, but somehow had never quite got round to it. It would be easier to remember, I thought, if only there was a church like this one at an appropriate point in each day's travel.

'Archangel Raphael accompany me as you did Tobias. Direct my feet so that I may travel in peace, safety and joy.'

I couldn't get a stamp for my passport in the church, the priest 'was in hospital with his chest' one of his concerned parishioners told me, adding, helpfully, that I could get one at the *Mairie* instead. Wheeling Roberts between the market stalls, I found myself a focus of interest in a way that had not happened anywhere else in France. People pointed me out to their neighbours, *'Une pèlerine'* – a pilgrim – I heard them remarking. Several came and asked me directly if I was going to Compostela, touching the scallop shell and murmuring *'un beau coquillage'*. They seemed so genuinely glad to greet a pilgrim that I thought they would also know the best place for me to have a good meal at a reasonable price. I was right, with no hesitation I was pointed to a serious-looking establishment in the centre of the market.

Chez Dumas had made no concessions to the age of the motor car as yet, and could easily have coped with the needs of a company of reasonably well to do pilgrims and their horses. Roberts looked totally out of place, alone among the empty stalls and the stone mangers of the cobbled coach yard. I was ushered into a dim, plain interior, varnished by time to a uniform creamy brown, and furnished with long oilcloth-covered tables and wooden benches. An old woman began to tell me what was on offer, but her accent was difficult to follow, and it seemed simpler to leave the choice to her. Had I not had a few hours of hard pedalling behind me this would have been a serious mistake, for even with a great hollow to fill, I had difficulty in coping with the succession of courses that arrived, each one of excellent quality and each a meal in itself – thick soup, stewed meat, a great plate of raw roast beef, mounds of vegetables, and a quite delicious fruit tart. As the tables slowly filled with other diners, I began to realise that I had been given twice as much as anyone else. I guessed that this was because of my pilgrim status, rather than because I might have looked hungry. I had read somewhere that it had once been the custom to give pilgrims double portions. I hadn't dreamt it still existed, but I was thankful that I had been able to acquit myself with honour.

St Sever had one further surprise for me. After I had been to the *Mairie*, chatted with the girls there and had my record stamped, the elderly usher, resplendent in green uniform, stopped me before I could ride off. Slipping a ten franc piece into my palm he said '*Pour un café sur la route, madame*'. Once in India, and again in Egypt, I have had gifts of money urged upon me by kindly men who had assumed that only extreme poverty could cause me to be riding around their respective countries on a bicycle. But since cycling is considered a noble sport in France, I did not think the doorman was moved by that sort of compassion. His alms I realised were a sort of sponsorship endorsing the pilgrimage in general. He considered I was doing something worthwhile, and by staking me to a coffee he had a share in the venture. It was a touching and kindly gesture, but it had its serious side too, dispelling the notion that I was an entirely free agent on this journey. And in fact the visit to St Sever was to prove a watershed; after it I was never again able to feel that going on pilgrimage to Santiago was something that concerned myself alone.

Heavy lunches need to be balanced by a nap or a gentle stroll; they certainly are not good for cycling, especially not when accompanied by a couple of glasses of full-bodied wine. Once more I found myself floundering feebly on the uphill sections, of which there were plenty, some of them quite formidable, and I began to be quite alarmed at the thought of the mountain barriers still to come. By five p.m., with a horrid, damp weather front closing in, I gave up the struggle, obtained permission from a friendly farmer to pitch my tent in the shelter of a belt of trees, and having decided to dispense with any further meals that day, read a little, and soon dropped into a much-needed, restorative sleep.

The next day showed no lifting of the cloud ceiling. The countryside was grey and melancholy like an early black and white film. I rather liked the period effect, with everything dripping, and the grass heavy with droplets of moisture. Even the cows, whose heads loomed over the wire fences eyeing me as I passed, had their long lashes beaded as though with tears. Under the grey concealing mist the contours of the land rose and fell continuously, and I tried to decide whether it was harder not to see the extent of the slopes that lay ahead, or a blessing. I was still unsure about this when I reached Orthez, a small town on the banks of the wide Gave de Pau. A few weak gleams of sunlight chose that moment to break through and immediately life in general seemed much more cheerful. It was further improved by a café in the main square opening its doors to the congregation who were beginning to file out of the church across the way. Studying the map over my coffee, I realised that I must be very close to a house where I was expected to call. The friendly Rigauds, who had entertained me in Cluis, had telephoned friends of theirs who had recently moved to a village on my route. It was on the spit of land in Aquitaine that lies between the two broad arms of the Gave, the northernmost of which, graced with a fortified medieval bridge, flowed darkly before me as I drank my coffee.

An hour later I was eating luncheon in a smart modern-ised farmhouse, the guest of André and Claire Legrain, an ex-airline pilot and his wife. Neither came from this part of France, but had chosen it for their retirement purely because it was close enough to the Pyrenees for them to go skiing with ease. They knew nothing of the Santiago pilgrimage or of the *Chemin de Compostelle* that passed so close to their door, though now they heard about it from me they realised the significance of names like *l'Hôpital d'Orion*, attached to a tiny village from which the great medieval buildings had long since vanished.

I spent a pleasant day with André and Claire, for they had the same warm gift of hospitality I had enjoyed with the Rigauds and made me feel very welcome. But I was surprised at just how novel it felt to be installed in a comfortable house after only two weeks of my spartan little tent. Sofas and armchairs seemed positively sybaritic, and as for the soft double bed I was to sleep in, compared with the narrow, inch-thick little mat I spent my nights on, it seemed ridiculous to suppose that the two things had anything in common. At this halfway point in the journey I was tired enough to appreciate a rest, but I cannot pretend that it was much of a mental relaxation. Claire spoke no English and André knew only as much as was required of an international pilot, so my erratic French was stretched to its utmost. Another couple came to dinner too, and as the conversation grew more animated it became only too easy to lose the thread altogether. I tried to make up for my lack of verbal contribution by looking attentive and intelligent, and fortunately this seemed to work, for every so often someone would say kindly 'Oh Bettina understands everything, it is only talking she finds difficult' – a misconception I did nothing to correct. I went to bed eventually, beautifully wined and dined but as exhausted as if I had just sat a gruelling examination paper.

The Legrains had kindly invited me to stay on for a day or two, but much as I liked them and would have enjoyed exploring this pretty part of Aquitaine in their company, now was not the time. After even so short a break I found myself eager to get back to the *Chemin de Compostelle*, to the more rigorous conditions, the close contact with nature, the periods of silence and the challenge of the road itself with its surprises and revelations. The pilgrimage, I was discovering imposed its own disciplines, together with its rewards, and turning aside to make visits did not really fit in with its demands.

I made an early start, and once again toiled up and down steep-sided countryside in a gentle warm downpour, and once I was thoroughly wet I quite enjoyed it, for the pretty cows with their long-fringed lashes, which I now knew to be a breed called *Blanche d'Aquitaine*, still poked their heads quizzically over the walls and fences as I passed.

Seeing the rare phenomenon of an open church at Sauveterre de Béarn, just before the crossing of the southern arm of the Gave, I seized the opportunity to get out of the rain for a while and have my record stamped. The priest, a born comic, said '*Beaucoup de descentes maintenant madame*,' adding after a short pause, '*et monts aussi, naturellement.*' He was quite right, the gradients increased as the symbol for a good view became more plentifully peppered over the map.

By mid-afternoon, when I was long past enjoying the rain, I arrived at Saint Palais, which from its name had led me to expect at least some vestiges of splendour and comfort. Alas for my expectations, I found it a down-at-heel place, made infinitely more so by the puddles, the soaked walls and the absence of lunch, the hour for which was long past. On the corner of the Avenue Gibraltar (nothing to do with the Rock, but a Basque corruption of the name St Saveur) I came upon the shabby priory of the Franciscans which seemed the oldest building there. I called in and my record was stamped and inscribed '*Paix et Joie*' with the

St James Peregrino

St James Matamoros

Bettina Leaving Vézelay

Cloister of the 'Twisted Pillar', Estella

Monastery church, San Juan de Ortega

Burgos Cathedral

Pilgrim door, Burgos

Granite cross near Hontanas

Fifteenth-century cross at Boadilla del Camino, complete with scallop shells

Basque equivalent underneath – which as far as I could make it out reads '*Bake ta Bozkario*'.

Gibraltar is the spot where the three routes, from Vézelay, Le Puy and Paris come together, and today a stele marks the junction. Had there been a place of refreshment instead, it would have seemed altogether more appropriate, but at least my arrival at the stele marked a halt in the rain, and I pressed on more cheerfully to Ostabat. Alas, here too I drew a blank, there was not even a village shop to sell a hungry bicyclist a bit of dry bread. Ostabat, the first pilgrim halt after the joining of the routes, had once boasted as many as twenty hospices. Now even the damp depressing-looking church was locked. Hopes were raised, however, when I was hailed in English from the steps of the building opposite, an *Hôtel de Ville* currently in the process of being rescued from total decay. 'Come and have a cup of coffee,' called a man, a Basque it transpired, who seemed to be in charge there. As soon as I was inside and had shed my dripping waterproof, the young man pushed the coffee jar aside after only the most cursory glance at it, remarking casually 'Only enough for a weak American brew', which made me suspect that I had been lured in under false pretences. Not that I could blame him. If I had to spend time in such a rain-sodden depressing place I too might be tempted to lure in passing travellers in order to relieve the monotony.

Aimery Picaud called the Basques 'A barbarous people', citing examples of their murderous customs, their perverted sexual practices and their gross eating habits. Their language came in for just as much condemnation: 'when you hear them speaking it is like the barking of dogs,' he wrote.

The origin of the Basques and their unique language remain a mystery, though Picaud thought they had descended from

the Scots, citing the similarity of their customs and appearance as proof – clearly he also harboured a low opinion of
the Caledonian race. If Frenchmen in general had shared
Picaud's views of the Basques, then it seemed to me no
wonder that I sensed an underlying hostility in my host.
In fact his conversation was blatantly confrontational.

'You know Brighton?' he began innocently enough, as
soon as I was seated. 'I been there with my punk group.' He
had since abandoned punk, he told me, except for the ring
in his ear, which he said he kept as a reminder, as well as
helping in his work with Basque youth groups. In answer to
my query, he said he had not liked England. 'Nasty country
with a bad record.' The British Empire was the worst of all
empires, apparently, especially in India. It had committed
outrages more horrible than the genocide of the American
Indians. Having dealt succinctly with the improbity of the
British Empire, he ran through a comprehensive list of
other empires, none of which had been other than bloody
and repressive. Only the Roman Empire was spared; for
that he had an unqualified admiration – though I couldn't
discover why. While I was still reeling from this sweeping
panorama of the sins of history, he launched into a political
lecture on the perfidy of both the French and the Spanish
in their dealings with his people. Their greatest iniquity,
I learnt, was in attempting to deny the Basques their
linguistic rights. By this time my head was spinning,
and I was more than keen to escape, but in the best
Ancient Mariner tradition, he barred my passage. I had
to listen to yet another lengthy discourse, this time on the
Basques' incomprehensible language (not constructed like
any other human tongue, he told me proudly). Finally I
seized my moment, and ducked smartly beneath the arm
he had firmly braced across the door frame.

The weather at least had improved during my unrefreshed stop. As I rode away from Ostabat and the one-sided airing of opinions, I saw with a sudden glad lifting of the spirits that the clouds were peeling off the high wooded slopes of the Pyrenees. It was only the briefest of glimpses, but enough to set the heart beating faster; further cloud fronts raced into the vacuum, sealing off the high peaks once again. By the time I reached the small town of St Jean-Pied-de-Port, nestling at the foot of the Pyrenees, the rain had penetrated my defences and was trickling coldly down my neck. There might have been no mountains at all, except for the swollen river, dangerously high and rushing and leaping over the boulders of its deep uneven bed. Remembering the exciting close-up view of the towering barrier ahead, however, I felt a shiver of excitement. Tonight I would sleep in this tiny walled and gated town that guarded the pass and tomorrow, God willing, I would be in Spain.

5

Beginning the Camino Francés

Crossing the Pyrenees from St Jean-Pied-de-Port, the traveller has a choice of two routes, both of which are steeped in history and legend. The Val Carlos Pass carries the main road, while the Pass Napoleon, once part of an old Roman road, is a rough track over the Col de Cize. Both will eventually bring the traveller to the door of monastery of Roncesvalles, but on the way there the Pass Napoleon climbs higher, enjoys more dramatic views and is the traditional route for pilgrims who shun the easier way – all compelling reasons for me to choose it, even if I would have to walk most of the way and manhandle Roberts over the rougher places. The solitude and the absence of the reek and roar of motor traffic would be reward enough, and if I could not make Roncesvalles in the day I had my tent and would enjoy camping up in the mountains.

My resolve was squashed with one word from Madame Debril 'Impossible'. Snow, rain and neglect, she said, had brought the Col de Cize track to a state where it was barely passable even for a fit well-equipped walker; a cyclist would be unlikely to get through much before late June. Indeed, she added darkly, the weather was so bad at present, I would be lucky not to have my way blocked by torrential rain, or even snow and blizzards on the Val Carlos road.

Madame Debril is invariably described in the guide books as a 'character of the road'. She is also St Jean-Pied-de-Port's authority on the *Camino*, as the pilgrim route is called from this point onward. *Camino Francés* – the French Road, to give it its full Spanish title – is an indication of how great a part France and its influential monasteries, particularly Cluny, played in establishing the St James pilgrimage. Five of Cluny's monks became Pope during the medieval period when Church rather than State was the dominant and unifying power of Western Europe. Although there were undoubtedly genuine pious reasons for promoting pilgrimages, it cannot be denied that by doing so they greatly bolstered the power, wealth and influence of the Church.

Such thoughts come readily to mind in Mme Debril's ancient house, which stands on the town's original main highway – a steep and cobbled street that runs up through the narrow defensive gates to the crowning citadel. For while it is impossible in this age of mass tourism that a town so placed would not become a tourist trap, St Jean-Pied-de-Port has not been offensively restored and retains a genuine feeling of the great age of religious journeys.

Madame Debril's dark, stone-flagged little office was crowded with memorabilia of the pilgrimage, amongst which lounged innumerable striped grey cats. Honours, mostly in the shape of silver scallop shells were propped up in their open velvet cases. These had been showered upon her by the various confraternities and organisations who have valued her help over the years. As the local representative of the Amis de St Jacques de Compostelle, the French equivalent of the Confraternity of St James, she had charge of the key to the refuge and was also responsible for issuing pilgrim passports to those who chose to begin their journey at St Jean-Pied-de-Port. But when I came to call on her that morning, I found a young Englishman in tears on her doorstep, having just been given the rough end of her tongue. He appeared a perfectly ordinary and reasonable person, a little over-sensitive perhaps, but then pilgrimage is an emotionally charged undertaking, and he had been several weeks on the road. He said that Mme Debril had been hostile from the outset, accusing him of not being a proper pilgrim, and had refused him the key to the refuge – the simple pilgrim accommodation maintained by some towns.

Forewarned, I was not too put out by my own reception, which was certainly less than friendly. 'Why had I not called the previous evening?' she snapped – though how she expected people to know what was a convenient time for her, when there was no notice about visiting hours on her door, I did not ascertain. Gradually, however, her mood changed and she became quite amiable, even complimenting me on the various stamps I had acquired in my pilgrim's passport, some of which were apparently quite rare – this I could well believe, remembering the problems I had encountered with locked churches.

Eventually the reason for Mme Debril's ill-humour was revealed; she had become a victim of the popularity of the Santiago pilgrimage and her own part in it. Fulfilling her voluntary obligations and keeping a record of passing pilgrims had not been an onerous task fifteen years before, when only a trickle of people were passing through on their way to Santiago. Many of her callers were academics researching the route, so it was all very interesting for Mme

Debril. But since the Spanish section – the *Camino Francés* – has been declared a European Heritage Trail there are too many people knocking at her door. She is reluctant to lay down her role, or to compromise with her execution of it. All the details she collects of the hundreds of pilgrims who do call (and she is perversely annoyed by the fact that there are probably just as many who do not) are later carefully transcribed in copperplate handwriting into special ledgers. She is also vigilant in her questioning of those requiring 'passports' in order to determine that they have the right motives. 'There are not many true pilgrims,' she told me. 'Most of them, particularly the Spanish, just want a free holiday. They turn up here with nothing, not even a pack. Proper pilgrims have something to identify them and they look like pilgrims.' This had been the young Englishman's mistake apparently; he had left his pack with a shopkeeper at the foot of the hill, and as he had no Confraternity papers or badges she had assumed he was another suspicious character.

'Drug addicts, thieves, layabouts, hippies.' Mme Debril's list of those who trod the road to Santiago, attempting to get their hands on the key to free lodgings, was like a page from Chaucer. I listened enthralled as, all unwittingly, she imbued my journey with magic once more. For it was life itself she was describing, full-blooded, whole and robust, and not some esoteric off-shoot of it, divorced from reality. As she was speaking I realised that if something worthwhile was to be achieved on my twentieth-century pilgrimage, it would be rooted in the ordinary, everyday world. The journey was not something outside time and reality, but an opportunity to look at the same realities from a different angle and in a different context. My ideas differed widely from those of Mme Debril, but when we parted, with expressions of cordiality on both sides, I thought the world, as well as the pilgrimage, would be the poorer without this irascible but passionately involved woman.

Much to my disappointment the rain had not cleared as I prepared to set out from St Jean-Pied-de-Port; it was falling in fact with the sort of dogged persistence that held out little hope of an early end to it. There would be no views as I slogged my way over the pass, and I wondered if I would do better to delay my departure until the next day. But there was no guarantee it would cease even then. Besides, I had found the hotel both noisy and expensive, and had already exhausted the sights of the town in a determined two-hour tour the previous evening. Much better to take the journey as it came, the bad with the good, I decided. Something worthwhile might emerge even from such dismal weather. I called in at the least touristy of the shops to buy some strong plastic bags to keep my shoes dry, having exhausted the stock I had brought with me. When I explained to the shopkeeper why I wanted them, he insisted on providing me with the best he had – no payment for a *pèlerine!* Customers and staff watched with interest as I moulded a bag over each shoe and put a rubber band around each ankle to hold them in place. My spare clothes and other luggage were already wrapped in plastic bags inside the panniers, a precaution I adopt now as a matter of course, for no luggage remains completely waterproof in prolonged rain. The handlebar bag is particularly vulnerable, as I discovered once in India when I was caught in a tropical downpour, and all my money, travellers' cheques, passport and other documents were reduced to pulp; so a separate bag is kept handy to pull over this at need.

Duly swathed and muffled in a Goretex top and trousers, with hood pulled well forward over my peaked beret to keep the water from streaming into my eyes and obscuring my vision, I set out from St Jean-Pied-de-Port with a sense of high adventure which, under the circumstances, might well have seemed misplaced. The rain, the fact that I certainly looked faintly ridiculous, and that I had a twenty-mile uphill stretch before me, most of which I would probably have to walk, made not a scrap of difference. This was the Val Carlos, the Valley of Charlemagne, where the legends of the 'Song of Roland' had their beginnings, and I had already caught the mood of it. Troubadours, it is said, accompanied bands of medieval pilgrims singing *chansons de geste* from the 'Song of Roland'. It was a time when the ideals of chivalry and religion had joined hands, each supporting the other, so that the two became somewhat confused. History found itself altered piecemeal in order to promote the myth that all great Christian kings and heroes had lived and died defending the Faith, rather than being primarily concerned with the preservation of their own realms and possessions. The Church itself was believed to have been instrumental in this bending of historical fact, and with precious little literacy outside of the monasteries this seems more than likely. I rather enjoyed the thought of monks and nuns composing these lovely, uplifting romances in their free time.

It is hard for us in an age of mass media to appreciate the importance of songs and stories in medieval Europe, and to realise the tremendous influence they had on the beliefs and ideas of the time. The songs of chivalry were on a par with the tales of the heroic deeds of St James himself, both as Slayer of Moors and as Pilgrim Miracle Worker. It must have been an extremely difficult time to separate fact from fiction, even had people wanted to. What is certain is that the Santiago pilgrims found the *chansons de geste* a source of inspiration. A forest of crosses was said to grace the top of the pass where I was headed, carried there by pilgrims to honour Charlemagne who had himself placed a cross there, legend claimed, and then had knelt in prayer, his face towards St James' shrine in distant Galicia. As the tomb of St James would not be discovered for another seventy years, this was as unlikely as the myth that Charlemagne was the first Santiago pilgrim. The same spot was also hallowed as the last stand of his great knight, Roland, slain by the perfidious Moors. But in reality, it was not Moors at all, but the wily Basques of Pamplona, fellow Christians in fact, who ambushed the rearguard of Charlemagne's army. And in slaying the cream of his palanquins, including Roland and Oliver, they were merely getting their own back on the army that had razed their city walls on its way to a mercenary engagement between two Moorish rulers.

But as I was soon to learn, faith is not necessarily based on dry historical fact, especially in relation to so celebrated a hero. And even nine centuries later, in full possession of the 'facts', it was the Charlemagne of popular legend who filled my thoughts as I rode away from St Jean, even though the road beside the sullen swollen river was evocative of nothing so romantic. A few drenched and dismal looking villages drooped over the further bank, and apart from that there was just the black streaming ribbon of tarmac and the dripping trees. I was still warm and dry in my waterproofs, however, and in the absence of a bona fide troubadour made my own music with a verse of 'He Who Would Valiant Be'.

The border came soon and suddenly with a right hand turn to cross the river. It proved to be a non-event. A French official waved me across from the shelter of his doorway, and as soon as I was over a Spanish official also gestured minimally for me to continue. Clearly female bicyclists were above suspicion, or not worth getting wet for. A sharp left brought me back on line and the climb proper began. I suppose there is some element of conceit in most of us. In me it takes the form of pretending that there is no real effort involved in tackling a steep incline, though I only do this when I think someone might be watching. I made a determined effort to push on until I was out of sight of the customs posts just in case someone was idly noting my progress from a window. By the time I judged I was out of sight, I was around the next bend, and heart, lungs and muscles had recovered a little from the initial shock of exertion. There was no reason not to try to make it to the next corner and having managed that I carried on to the next one. At each bend the gradient steepened, and I thought I had reached my limit, and I would have to get off and walk. But every time a fresh burst of energy got me round it, and then as the gradient eased a little I found myself able to continue to the next corner. The only traffic was an occasional lorry, piled high with tree trunks, and also grinding its way with difficulty around the hairpin bends. The knowledge that I was not alone in finding the going tough was a further spur to effort.

About halfway up I had the distinct impression that it was St James himself who was pushing me on from behind. It wasn't a blinding revelation, or anything that seemed particularly out of the ordinary at that stage, just the sense of a kindly, practical, no-nonsense sort of character lending a helping hand; a feeling that grew on me gradually. Several times I was almost on the point of turning around to thank him, and it was only later that I thought of this as odd, for I did not for a moment believe that St James had ever set foot in Spain, dead or alive.

But there are strange powers attached to places that

cannot be rationally explained. Certain tiny islands in the Hebrides where the Celtic monks built their cells have this aura; the ruins of the Monastery of Sumela in Eastern Turkey, Lindisfarne and many other similar holy places also possess it strongly. Equally, the sites of really hideous deeds appear to have the reverse of it, and to repel people, even those who have come there by chance and have no idea of the grim events that were enacted in the place. The sense of a benign presence that I experienced on the ascent of the Pyrenees was not uncommon I was to discover later. Lots of modern pilgrims have felt it too, and although equally sceptical have, without thinking, called it St James. And if this is a case of balancing belief and disbelief in either hand, so be it.

In spite of the rain, which continued off and on but never stopped long enough for me to remove my rain gear, the climb out of the green valley of Charlemagne was beautiful. The road loops through broad-leaved forest for most of the way, and the acres of tender green leaves gave a feeling of abundance and renewal. But it was the climb itself that brought the real pleasure. In spite of the help from St James I was stretched to the full, and whether or not it is true that hard physical exercise causes the brain to produce endorphin which has the same effect as a euphoric drug, I certainly felt elated. By the time I reached the summit at Ibeñata, where Roland and Oliver fell and where the medieval age of romance and chivalry had its beginnings, I felt on top of the world in more ways than one.

This could well have proved my undoing, for overheated as I was from the climb, I should have had the sense to seek shelter, or at least to pile on more clothes to counteract the drop in body temperature that follows closely upon such exertion. Instead I wandered about the bleak rain-drenched open summit, trying to make out from the few stones left in the turf, the ground plan of the monastery Charlemagne had founded at the historical site.

Coming up the sheltered eastern face of the mountain I had been unaware of the strong westerly wind, but in this exposed spot it blew with the mournful urgency of Roland's famous horn.

On that fateful day in 778 AD he had blown it to no avail, for Charlemagne and the main body of the army were already down in the valley, unable to come back to the aid of the rearguard in time. The conditions, I thought, were absolutely right for filming the scene: the grey Celtic light, the rain slanting viciously on the wind and the huge strewn boulders, any of which could have been the fragments of the one split by Roland's mighty sword as he vainly sought to smash the blade before he died.

I was drenched through and shivering before I realised that the conditions were also right for the onset of pneumonia. Fortunately Roncesvalles is only a short distance beyond the summit, but even so I was almost blinded by the sharp horizontal rain before I got down to it. The acres of depressing corrugated zinc which roofs the monastery which met me as I turned the corner were in no sense a disappointment, for they spelled welcome shelter.

A small inn, *Casa Sabina*, stood beside the sprawling monastic buildings and as I came to it first I went in. My temperature had dropped even lower on the short descent and the hot radiator in the tiny foyer was as welcoming as all the delights of the Alhambra. While I was hugging it, feeling distinctly the worse for wear, a young woman appeared from the kitchen to see who had come in. Discovering that I was English she went to fetch her father. By this time I could recognise a Basque by the outsize circumference of his black beret, and this small white-haired man was wearing one which seemed wider than he was high. He tut-tutted at my damp bedraggled appearance, and without a word poured me a glass of dark red wine. In my depleted state it raced through my veins with the speed of light and had an even more intoxicating effect than the euphoria of the climb. I stopped shivering almost at once.

An hour or so later, after I had eaten a large portion of red bean stew laced with peppers and sausage, and had finished the bottle of delicious Navarrese wine with my host, I decided that Aimery Picaud must have based his condemnation of the Basque race on a very limited field of observation. It seemed to me that their wine, their food and their company were decidedly civilised, not to say, merry.

The monastery of Roncesvalles took on decidedly more interesting appearance after this protracted relaxing lunch. It is true that the present buildings are an odd mixture of styles and periods, and are not in the best of repair, and that the steeply pitched zinc roofs are totally out of keeping with its dignity, yet it has something – atmosphere certainly. Whether one approves of its architecture or not, its setting among mature beech woods is undoubtedly lovely and its history is impressive. An Augustinian foundation, it was established here by a bishop of Pamplona in the twelfth century in order to maintain one of the most important pilgrim hospices of the whole route. Poised on the threshold of Spain – St James' own chosen land – linked through Charlemagne and Roland to the Christian Reconquest, and coming after one of the most arduous stretches of the route, Roncesvalles couldn't help but assume a special role in the pilgrim's itinerary. It is still one of the most emotionally charged positions of the *Camino*.

In its heyday it was like a small city and the pilgrims who made it there could relax for three days in what for the time was heady luxury. There was a hospital for the sick as well as an apothecary's services for those with minor ailments. There were separate dormitories for men and women, furnished with beds instead of simply having straw strewn on flagstones. Baths were available, and there were cobblers to repair the pilgrims' footwear and blacksmiths to shoe the horses of the wealthier pilgrims. For their spiritual comfort a miraculous statue of the Virgin (made not by human hands and discovered through the intermediary of a stag with a star shining between his antlers) graced the church. A funerary chapel believed to contain the bodies of Charlemagne's fallen heroes offered a further focus for devotion. This together with the pilgrims' own chapel at the gate of the monastery are the oldest buildings of the present-day complex.

I leaned Roberts against the wall of the long nineteenth-century building which houses the monks' quarters, the treasury and various offices and went to find out if I could stay in the *refugio*. After a short wait the father on duty, Don Javier Navarro, another Basque, emerged clad in modern dress, complete with cartwheel beret, and I was taken to a small office to fill in a questionnaire. Apart from the usual questions of age, sex, nationality, religion, point of departure etcetera, there was 'motive for journey?'. This gave me some difficulty, for five possible reasons were suggested – religious, spiritual, recreational, cultural and sporting. Don Javier urged me to tick as many of these motivations as I thought appropriate. When I thought about them I could see that almost all had some bearing on why I was cycling to Santiago, although had I not been presented with the list I might not have started thinking of the subtle differences between such words as spiritual and religious. The only one I didn't tick was 'sporting', which I rejected because at the time I could only think of sport as an organised activity like football or the Tour de France, and that didn't seem appropriate to a lone traveller. But later, mulling it over, it seemed to me that risk and adventure are as essential to sport as they are to pilgrimage, so in that sense all the motives had some bearing on the journey, as well as others that were not included – like curiosity and love of travel.

My form filling being judged satisfactory, the father shook my hand and gave me a new pilgrim's passport, impressively entitled *Credencial del Peregrino* which had been duly stamped and signed. This he explained would enable me to lodge at the *refugios* in the towns and villages along the way. It would also entitle me to meals at reduced prices in certain places (I never discovered any of these places, but I was also never in such a state of penury as to need them). On arrival in Santiago, he added, I would be examined by the cathedral authorities and if I was found worthy would be granted my *Compostela* and would then be able to celebrate with free meals at the prestigious Hospital de los Reyes Católicos, built for pilgrims by King Ferdinand and Queen Isabella and which was now a five-star hotel.

The little ceremony over, Don Javier prepared to escort me to the monastery's *refugio*. Unfortunately the excess of exercise and the heavy red wine at lunch had made my knees rather rubbery. As I collected Roberts it somehow got off balance and fell over with both the little monk and myself mixed up with it. After we had picked ourselves up, Don Javier firmly took charge of the cycle, wheeling it along with great caution and at arm's length. A colleague called out something to him which seemed to be in the nature of a jest at the unusual sight, and he replied with a backward nod at me – that the 'poor thing was exhausted with her journey'. Which was certainly better than being suspected of being over the limit, even if I wouldn't have been the first pilgrim to have had a glass too many.

The Roncesvalles *refugio* does not live up to the reputation for comfort of its medieval forerunner. It is housed in an older part of the complex from the monks' quarters, on a higher level and approached through ancient, draughty stone corridors roughly floored with cobble stones laid in primitive, fan-shaped patterning. An oak stairway, its thick wide planks sloping with age, led to two dormitories. Both were closely packed with three-tiered metal bunks, and each was illuminated by a single tiny window. There was a small inner hall furnished with a long table and benches, where a few naked, low-wattage lightbulbs pierced the gloom. An archaic, lethal-looking gas water-heater hung on a wall of the tiny kitchen, which otherwise contained nothing but two saucepans with holes in them, a couple of chairs and an empty hearth. The monk advanced a match to the geyser which immediately exploded with a loud and ominous report. Bravely he tried again, and with admirable perseverance, finally persuaded it to function; after which he was able to demonstrate proudly that there was now a supply of hot water to the spartan little washroom next door. Informing me that mass would be at eight, I was then left to my own devices.

In spite of the cold and the general lack of comfort I felt there was a sense of rightness about the pilgrim lodgings in Roncesvalles that was not entirely of the hair shirt variety. The chilly air and the dank weather could not dispel the romance of centuries. If threads of troubadour song had drifted about the rafters, together with the strains of a distant hurdy-gurdy it would not have seemed out of place. From the tiny window of the dormitory I could see out over a large part of the monastery site. The rain was still lashing down on the undeniably grim corrugated roofs. Beneath them, by contrast, the worked stone of the walls assumed a delicacy and beauty, particularly the west wall of the collegiate church with its lovely rose window. The whole place was redolent of the times and events that had shaped it. Vulnerable and threadbare now, it had faced twelve centuries of changing fortunes, including the rabble of scores of barbarous armies passing through on their missions of invasion and reprisal. That it had survived all this and still offered shelter to the pilgrims of today's materialistic world seemed little short of miraculous. I felt it an honour to be there, and donning my damp waterproofs went out to explore the rest of it.

The mouldering arcades eventually led me to a dank late Gothic cloister of modest size whose wet upper walls sprouted clumps of varied plant life. A refurbished chapter-house of an earlier period led off one aisle. It had been adapted some decades before to contain the tomb of Sancho VII, known as The Strong, and famous for his victory over the Moors at the decisive battle of Navas de Tolosa in 1212. The huge marble tomb in the centre of the floor testified to the claim that Sancho was of great height. His corresponding strength was celebrated by two pieces of rusty broken chain hanging on the wall, parts of the chain which had protected the Moorish king's tent, and which Sancho had hacked through with his great sword. After the battle chains were incorporated into the arms of Navarre.

Both the funerary church and the tiny pilgrims' chapel at the entrance were locked, but I was able to have a quick look at the most famous of Roncesvalles' treasures,

'Charlemagne's chess set'. This was by special grace and favour of the young woman who had the key to the treasury and who was reluctant to open it except by special appointment, and then only to large bus parties. Her main job, she said, was getting the fathers' meals, and she couldn't be everywhere at once. She had the parlour floor still to finish, but if I could wait she would try and let me in for five minutes after that. Treating it as an exercise in patience (a virtue in which I am sorely lacking) I kicked my heels for half an hour, not daring to stray in case I missed the moment. When I was summoned, she was strict about sparing only the allotted five minutes, and of the rest of the room I had only a vague impression of pictures, monstrances and chalices, bright with gilt and enamel. Charlemagne's priceless reliquary was enamelled too, squared like a chessboard but with crystal-covered spaces for the fragments of the True Cross it contained, which themselves were in the form of a cross. It was a thing lovingly and skilfully crafted, but that says little about the impact it makes. If it was fashioned for Charlemagne sometime in the eighth century, it was much nearer to the extraordinary events it celebrated than was my century to Charlemagne's. Easy enough now to be cynical about the many thousands of fragments claimed to be from the 'True Cross', but that is also to ignore the deep sense of devotion that such things inspired. It was something of that devotion that I felt I'd glimpsed as I gazed at Charlemagne's chess set.

Back in the pilgrim quarters I found I was no longer alone. The other dormitory was bustling with an excited party of twenty or so Spanish men and women of various ages who had just arrived by bus, and who were setting off next day to begin their walk to Santiago. My dormitory was swelled by two Belgians, a woman of my own age who with her niece, Eva, was also planning to walk the five hundred miles to the shrine of St James. But they had already toiled up the Col de Cize route from St Jean-Pied-de-Port and were drenched through and very tired, particularly the older woman, Sophie. They confirmed all Mme Debril had said of the track: it was in a parlous state, two feet under water in places, and it had taken them more than ten hours to complete the ascent. It was a hard trek for a first day, and their feet were blistered. They hadn't discovered the efficacy of plastic bags either, so most of the contents of their rucksacks which could absorb water were sodden, spare clothes, bread and books included. The dormitory was strewn with their sopping garments and boots, and I thought the most helpful thing I could do would be to light a fire. I'd noticed that the hearth in the kitchen had a pile of brushwood beside it ready, it seemed, for just such a need. But first, in the absence of a glass of restoring wine from *Casa Sabina*, I offered them a shot of my emergency whisky as a sovereign remedy for warding off chills. The fire was got going after a fashion, and with all the assorted company squashed into the smoky little space drinking tea brewed on our stoves, it was comfortably warm. The Spanish didn't know much French or English and like most groups at the beginning of a venture they had plenty to talk about among themselves, but they took the trouble to smile at us, and to include us when they passed biscuits or chocolate around, so that there was an atmosphere of conviviality in the refuge.

The Belgians and I swapped stories in a satisfyingly polyglot mixture of English, French and Dutch. I learned that it was Sophie's second attempt to walk to Santiago. The previous year, she had got about a third of the way before being admitted to hospital with a serious chest infection. Her husband had to be sent for to take her home, and he had only agreed to her setting out again, she confided, because Eva, her niece, who was a student nurse, had agreed to come with her. But what had caused her to set her sights on Santiago in the first place I never really discovered. She was not religious in any accepted sense of the word, nor did she seem to be looking for answers to the great quandaries of human existence. She was not drawn by the marvellous church architecture on the route, nor was she a particularly athletic type who enjoyed the outdoor life for its own sake. She didn't even like Spaniards very much, finding them far too noisy. 'You wait,' she said to me in a darkly conspiratorial whisper. 'This lot haven't even walked today, they'll be talking and laughing until one or two in the morning, keeping us all awake.' And yet even such blunt un-Christian remarks could not veil the essential attractive honesty and warmth which were her chief characteristics. When in fact the Spanish turned out to be totally inoffensive and to have retired to bed by ten o'clock, it was Sophie herself who pointed this out, and who castigated herself for her uncharitable remarks about them.

It was clear to anyone that Sophie was a woman of determination – headstrong some would call her. She had set out to achieve a particular goal, and she was going to keep at it if it took her a lifetime. Eva confided to me that her aunt suffered frequent bronchial attacks and was not strong. No one in the family expected her to succeed in getting to Santiago, she said, but no one could dissuade her from attempting it either.

When I wakened during the night listening to the small unfamiliar creaks and murmurs of the old buildings, I found I was thinking about Keats' 'Ode on a Grecian Urn'. It had come to mind because of what Eva had told me about her aunt. The figures on the Grecian urn had been captured by the potter at the moment of reaching out towards some particularly desired thing; like the lover approaching his beloved. Keats sees this frozen intensity of passion that never reaches its goal as a blessed state:

'. . . yet do not grieve . . . though thou hast not thy bliss, forever wilt thou love and she be fair.'

I thought that Sophie too would probably never quite achieve her goal, but that the urge to walk to Santiago would always be there, adding something special to her life, something big to look forward to, to plan for, to set out towards year after year. As many have discovered it is not the arrival that matters, but the journey itself.

6

Across Navarre

In spite of the expectation of an effortless glide down the southern side of the Pyrenees – a delightful prospect for any bicycle traveller – I found myself reluctant to leave Roncesvalles the following morning. I was aware that I had come upon something special there, particularly during the previous evening's mass, which I wasn't eager to lose.

The collegiate church of Roncesvalles is one of the most satisfactory settings that could be found for a pilgrim mass. For no matter how many times its walls have been rebuilt, they still enclose the spot from which for eight hundred years and more an unbroken stream of particularly heartfelt prayer has arisen. A traveller arriving cold and weary at Roncesvalles is extremely thankful for its existence, as I now knew from personal experience. But the gratitude of a modern traveller can be only a fraction of what medieval pilgrims felt. Don Javier told me that one of the chief duties of the monks of Roncesvalles (a duty continued to the present day) was to pray for the souls of the thousands of pilgrims who died on their way to Santiago. The bones of many who were never to reach St James' Shrine lie in the underground ossuary beneath the funeral chapel at the gate, the victims of wolves, thieves, warring bands, or of the notorious mountain mists in which many pilgrims lost their way and perished of cold and hunger. This last hazard claimed so many victims that a bell used to be rung at Ibañeta in an attempt to guide them to safety. The worship and thanksgiving offered up by those who had survived all these dangers must have been especially fervent, and it would have been strange if this had not been reflected in the aura of the place.

From the description in my guide book I had been expecting to find a church crudely restored and shorn of all atmosphere. But to me it appeared exactly the reverse of this, though I must admit that coming from the icy dormitories to a warmly heated interior did immediately predispose me in its favour. Possibly I am no purist either, for I prefer buildings to be in good repair, with the stonework cleaned and broken pieces replaced. After all, in previous centuries, an army of itinerant stone masons, glass workers, carpenters and jobbing craftsmen moved continuously from church to church, cathedral to cathedral, patching and renewing the fabric as required.

The original building is French Gothic circa 1200, a three-aisled basilica, with triforium galleries and delicate pillars. I particularly liked the subdued concealed lighting which created a gentle, rather mysterious effect, very suitable for a church and I thought that if electricity had been available to the original builders they might well have used it in the same way. Above the high altar stands the famous statue of the miraculous Virgin of the Sorrows with her diamond tears. The infant Jesus appears to be trying to escape from her arms, and she, knowing his destiny, is attempting to hold on to him for a little while longer. Initially I was not much taken with this focus of pilgrim devotion, possibly because miraculous statues have not played any part in my religious upbringing, any more than have relics. But it could also be that the silver sheathing which covers both Virgin and Child prevents one seeing the power of the original work. The more I looked at it, however, the more I liked it, especially the dark uncovered face of the Mother which had an enigmatic quality that I thought would not pall half as quickly as that of the Mona Lisa.

I had asked Don Javier if it was all right for me, as an Anglican, to receive communion at their Roman Catholic mass and had been assured that it was. I always find it best to clear this point beforehand, as strictly speaking the celebration is quite different for Catholics and Protestants due to the thorny question of transubstantiation – does the bread and wine become the body and blood of Christ as Catholics teach? Or is it purely a symbolic memorial? Some clerics object strongly to Protestants and Catholics partaking fully in each other's celebration. I find no problem personally, and the High Anglican Church takes a middle position on the issue, holding both ideas without trying to make literal sense of them.

The congregation was about fifty strong, half pilgrims and half local people who either worked or lived at the monastery. All were Roman Catholics except for the Belgians and me. The Belgians did not belong to any church and so were not troubled by any theological hair-splitting. They believed in God, they said, kept an open mind about Jesus, and thought most religions were saying much the same thing anyway. They did their best to follow the unfamiliar movements of the mass, kneeling when the rest of us knelt and crossing themselves at the appropriate places. When we came to the Passing of the Peace and everyone turned to greet their neighbour, Sophie was clearly moved, and went around the whole congregation shaking everyone's hand. Which just goes to show how someone new to a ritual can often bring a fresh breath of life to it. Of course, if the whole congregation followed suit and insisted on embracing everyone present a service could take a very long time indeed. When the rest of us went forward to receive communion, Sophie and Eva went too. Possibly neither of them had ever been baptised, and I knew they had not been confirmed, but somehow that too did not seem to matter at Roncesvalles. What did matter was the atmosphere of acceptance and peace, the sense of unity in a diverse congregation of people who had come together in a very special place.

After the mass all the pilgrims were called up to the altar rail and the officiating father blessed us, group by group, in our various languages, using the ancient prayers of the 'Pilgrim's Itinerarium'.

'. . . O God who didst bring thy servant Abraham out of Ur of the Chaldeans, and didst preserve him unhurt through all the paths of his pilgrimage, vouchsafe we beseech Thee to keep these Thy servants. Be unto them a well-wishing in their setting out, a solace on the way, a shade in heat, a covering in the wind and cold, a fortress in adversity . . . that under Thy guidance they may happily reach the end of their journey . . .'

And when these solemn and deeply inspiring prayers were concluded, the priest opened his arms out wide to us all and said very simply, in Spanish that even I could understand, 'Pilgrims, remember to pray for us when you come to Santiago de Compostela.'

I think it was this moment that finally made a real if reluctant pilgrim of me. The entreaty 'Priez pour nous' had moved me in France, but in the atmosphere of Roncesvalles it had a compulsion that I could not ignore. It got me off the fence. It was the point at which I had to admit that this was not like any other journey; that no matter how light-heartedly I had set out, I had made a commitment more embracing than simply arriving at a specified destination. What that commitment might mean I didn't really know at this stage, but accepting that I had made it was somehow comforting, like laying down a burden.

When I woke, Roncesvalles was wrapped in one of its infamous mists and appeared more medieval than ever. Sophie's and Eva's wet clothes were still dripping disconsolately onto the rough boards, and they decided to stay warmly cocooned in their sleeping bags until Casa Sabina opened its doors for breakfast. I could well have followed their example, but reluctant though I was to leave both Roncesvalles and the first fellow pilgrims of the journey, it seemed best to get going. I didn't want breakfast because I was still recovering from supper. At home I have my evening meal between six and seven, and it had been ten the previous night before Gabriel brought the three of us his Navarrese speciality of mountain trout cooked with a thick slice of ham inside. It had proved delicious but had also given me a wakeful night. Clearly I was going to have to adjust to a different timetable in Spain. In the meantime I wouldn't need to think about eating again until I was down in Pamplona.

The saintly, quiet Spanish group had got themselves together and departed before I had even washed myself at the spartan sink. I caught up with them just before they turned off the road and we called suitable pilgrim salutations to each other before disappearing into the mist.

From the Spanish border the Santiago pilgrim route, unlike that from Vézelay, is precisely laid down, though I gathered it was still very easy to get lost in places. It would not be possible for me to travel the original path the whole way, as quite large stretches of it are very rough or water logged, suitable only for walking, and not even a mountain bicycle or a large-tyred hybrid like Roberts can get through, especially not a laden one. Wherever possible, however, I would go off the road onto the true pilgrim track, and in any case, all the main villages and towns of the *Camino* would be on my route, as road and path come together at these points.

Painted yellow arrows were what I had to look out for, these and the more formal scallop shell signposts and information boards set up by official bodies along the highways showed the course of the *Camino* across the Spanish countryside. The first yellow arrow roughly painted on a rock marked the turn-off down which my Roncesvalles companions had now vanished into the mist.

With a marvellous north wind at my back I was soon below the swirling cloud and was speeding joyously down the mountainside, only to have to toil up the next ridge back to the same height as Roncesvalles. This pattern of down and up again continued for some time, though it was mainly down, until I reached Pamplona, the Basque capital – Hemingway country.

Pamplona was built by Pompey in the first century BC when the Romans were trying to subdue the restless Basques. A city with a long and interesting history, it did not at first prove a good experience for me. Maybe the Basques of Pamplona only really come alive when the bulls are run through the streets before going to meet their deaths in the bull-ring in the heat of a July afternoon. A traveller's view of a place is to some extent coloured by the people they chance to meet there, and no one seemed to be smiling in Pamplona when I arrived. The day was grey which did nothing for the local stone, and worst of all, the famous cathedral was firmly locked. This last would not have mattered quite so much, in spite of the tempting things I had read about it, had not a notice on the gate firmly alleged that it would open in an hour or two. I hung about for ages after the stated time, but still every door and gate remained locked. Finally thinking I was going mad, or did not know how to interpret the notice, I stopped a passing priest to ask him to elucidate the matter. The man reacted rather like the White Rabbit in *Alice*, continuing to read his breviary as he quickened his pace, acknowledging that he had heard my request only by the unsmiling and dismissive gesture of a faintly raised chin in the direction of the misleading notice. It was the final straw. I shook the dust of Pamplona metaphorically from my tyres and returned to the *Camino*. At least it was not raining!

What reprieved the day was a village on the outskirts of Pamplona where I spent the night. Cizur Menor is on a small hill and boasts the remains of a stronghold of the Knights of St John, an order more usually associated with the Crusades and the pilgrimage to Jerusalem. But, together with the Knights Templar, the Hospitallers had also defended the Santiago pilgrimage route, especially after the thirteenth century when Saladin had finally routed the last of the Crusaders from Acre, their sole remaining stronghold in the Holy Land. There was little to see of this fragment of their long eventful history, but in any case the main

85

attraction of Cizur Menor for me was the erstwhile hen house of a local wealthy family.

The person responsible for transforming this commodious shed into superior lodgings for twelve pilgrims was Isbil Roncal, a lady as immersed in the history and politics of the *Camino* as Mme Debril in St Jean-Pied-de-Port. Isbil also beavers away on committees for improving the route, and was just about to drive into town to attend a special convention on the subject as I arrived. When I told her how frustrating my visit to Pamplona had been she insisted on taking me back in with her so that a real live pilgrim could be produced to tell various influential people present of how bad an impression the locked cathedral made. Apparently the opening hours were a perennial subject of contention in Pamplona. I had no wish to be dragged into local politics, but was powerless against Isbil's whirlwind enthusiasm. Almost before I knew what was happening, Roberts was locked up in the *refugio* and I, still unwashed and sweaty in my pilgrim's garb, was sitting in a large opulent hall, full of well-dressed people.

Fortunately there proved to be no free slot where Isbil could produce her pilgrim like a rabbit from a hat. She also realised, kind considerate person that she really was, that since I knew no Spanish, I was not getting a great deal out of the proceedings and she took me off on a tour of Pamplona instead.

But even with Isbil's help, the cathedral remained resolutely shut, and the few Spanish Baroque churches that were open did little more than offer me a somewhat greater understanding of El Greco's world. I would need to feel my way slowly into Spanish ecclesiastical architecture, particularly its statuary, which was all quite new to me.

What I enjoyed more immediately were the small glimpses

into Spanish life that Isbil gave me. We went to a lottery stall to check if she had won anything that week. Clearly she had no shortage of funds, but I was to find that nearly everyone, rich and poor alike, played one or another of the many lotteries in Spain as a normal part of life. It seemed considerably more casual than football pools, a matter of pure chance. After consulting a computer, the clerk told Isbil she had won the equivalent of about half her monthly stake. This was her usual pattern apparently, she collected about half to three-quarters of what she paid out and immediately bought more tickets. She said the stake was trifling and the reward didn't matter in the least; it was the anticipation that gave her a great deal of pleasure.

Another revelation came when we were walking along a straight narrow pavement with the high walls of the convent school on one side, which Isbil had attended as a girl. It was part of the route where the bulls are run through the town on their way to the bull-ring. 'It is so wonderful to see them, so wonderful and so sad too, because they are so beautiful, and you know that in the afternoon they will die,' she said, trying to explain to me the beauty and satisfaction she found in Pamplona's famous yearly bull-fighting festival. It seemed strange to hear the proceedings extolled from the victims' side rather than the matadors', but perhaps it said something about the Spanish character. To judge by the gory effigies of tortured saints and the severely realistic crucifixions in the churches we had just visited, Spanish Christianity places a special emphasis on suffering. The Spanish Inquisition was the most fanatical branch of that most sinister institution, the Holy Office, with a reputation for cruelty and zeal that outstripped all others. That it succeeded so well in Spain was because of its popularity with the Spanish people. The *autos da fé* (acts of faith) at which the punishment of convicted heretics was carried out publicly, usually by burning at the stake, were great national festivals. Perhaps with the Inquisition abolished, the bull-fight fulfils some deep need in the Spanish psyche. Certainly, listening to Isbil extolling it made me think of how easy it is in the twentieth century to forget that suffering and sacrifice are at the heart of the Christian faith.

Back at Cizur Menor, Isbil settled me in and collected the small charge for the night's stay. Her talk was so full of pilgrims and their doings that it occurred to me to wonder if the pretty and self-consciously rustic little *refugio* did not fulfil some unrealised childhood dream of hers. It was curiously reminiscent of a doll's house, carefully constructed at no small expense, and with every item of furniture chosen to be in keeping with the image. It had everything that twelve well-behaved house-trained little pilgrims could possibly want, a set for each, right down to their twelve, highly polished knives, forks and spoons. Comfortable though it certainly was, it also had a somewhat zany feel to it and I found myself toying with macabre ideas – like being confronted by a row of eleven stiff little wooden pilgrims and knowing that I made up the set, or suddenly finding a gigantic child's eye peering in through a window.

No nightmares disturbed my sleep however. In the peace of my neatly curtained wooden bunk bed I read the 'Office of Compline' with its appropriate opening of 'May the Lord Almighty grant us a quiet night and a perfect end' and was aware of nothing after that until six the following morning.

Estella was to be the next night's stop. Not a demanding journey, for even with detours it would only be about thirty-five miles. But there were places I wanted to see along the way, and in any case I had no wish to hurry. I still had two weeks in which to reach Santiago which was less than five hundred miles distant at this point.

Isbil had recommended I start with a detour in order to avoid the horrors of a particularly villainous stretch of main road, notorious for martyring modern pilgrims. Accordingly I set off into a landscape of low, rolling, grassy hills dotted about with strange-looking industrial machinery used, I decided eventually, for some sort of quarrying purposes. Heavy lorries transporting aggregate rumbled past occasionally, requiring the whole width of the unfenced lanes that had become crazed and pot-holed by their great weight. I found it sensible to take to the grass verge as soon as I heard them approaching. With all the stopping and the ups and downs it would have been hard work had the stiff little wind not still been at my back.

A short spell on the death-defying N 111 convinced me of how wise Isbil had been to suggest the route which had kept me off it until this point. Praying hard to St Raphael, the special guardian angel of travellers, I survived a few kilometres in safety until I reached my next detour where minor roads would connect me with the last few kilometres of the fourth of the classic routes to Santiago, before it joined the other three at Puente la Reina, the Queen's Bridge. This was the route from Arles that was used by those coming from the south of France and from Italy. Alone of all the routes, it crosses the Pyrenees by the Somport Pass. Apart from escaping the N 111, I had chosen to cycle these last few miles of it in order to see the church of Eunate, another famous burial place for medieval pilgrims.

The lovely little octagonal Romanesque church is situated in solitary splendour among wide flat grain fields, newly green at this season. The gently curved cupola capped with an open bell turret and a small rounded tower known as a lantern of the dead, were sharply delineated against wide blue skies, and in the open landscape the delicate building had a suitable melancholy air that went well with its role.

These round or octagonal churches were modelled on the Holy Sepulchre in Jerusalem and were usually the work of the Knights Templar. But although the Templars flourished in Navarre, many guide books wrongly ascribe this church to them. It was, in fact, built by the Knights of St John of Jerusalem, the Hospitallers, and was once part of a pilgrim hospital. I could see little resemblance to the Holy Sepulchre, apart from the basic shape. The lovely external arcading forming a cloister all around Eunate gives it a unique delicate quality, earning for it its Basque name meaning 'Church of the Hundred Doorways'.

As I sat there enjoying the beauty and serenity of the place, and thinking that it would be a good idea to boil the kettle for a cup of coffee, a bus drew up and a class of ten-year-old Spanish school children poured out chirping like a bunch of excited starlings. It was a sudden and rude return to the twentieth century, and their keen interest in me after their teacher pointed me out as a *peregrina* – a live pilgrim specimen for their history lesson – was anything but welcome. But just in time I remembered the moment at Roncesvalles when I had accepted the role; this too was clearly a part of it. Nor was it any use worrying about what sort of figure I cut for these young Spaniards. At least they could see at first hand that there were people who still journeyed the ancient road by other means than fast cars and buses. To judge from the cans of pop and the bags of crisps which were thrust towards me from all directions, I concluded I had not come across too badly. Numerous snapshots were also taken of the laden Roberts with his scallop shells, and a tape recorder was produced for an interview. Unfortunately the language barrier proved too much for both children and me, and their teacher had to extract the information in French. It was my age that seemed to impress them most. 'Over fifty and cycling all the way from England!' their teacher translated. The round eyes and exclamations of amazement said it all.

Two miles after Eunate and I had come to Obanos and the joining of the four ways. From this point a single road continues to the shrine of Santiago, and to mark the significance of the place a modern statue of a medieval pilgrim stands facing the distant goal. Barely another mile travelled and yet a further delight for the eyes. This is the Puente la Reina, the medieval bridge spanning the River Arga. A charitable queen had it built sometime in the eleventh century out of pity for the pilgrims who found the river a great hazard with its flash floods and villainous ferrymen. There is nothing in the least ornate about the bridge, just a slender bow of stone rising high to cross the water in one clean, pure line. But it made me catch my breath in wonder that something so simply utilitarian could achieve so satisfying a form.

So important was the bridge as a crossing place that by the thirteenth century a walled town, also called Puente la Reina had sprung up beside it, bustling with trade. The modern road by-passes this, but the Road to Santiago enters through a vaulted passageway that becomes the narrow main street, the Calle Mayor. Like a member of a masonic cult I was directed by special signs, in my case yellow arrows handpainted on kerbstones or on the corners of walls, inconspicuous but charged with significance. They joined me to the invisible army that had trodden these cobble stones before me, and I found the way suddenly much expanded and full of meaning. The heavily shadowed alleyway runs between Romanesque churches and houses with Gothic doorways. Nothing is obviously restored or preserved which makes it all the more redolent of the Middle Ages. A final arrow pointed me out through the walls and onto the narrow Puente la Reina, but had even one of the town's famous churches been open I could have spent at least half a day there.

It was the same problem at Cirauqui, a small hilltop village a little further along. Cirauqui doesn't actually straddle the route, the path skirts around the bottom of it, but nonetheless it is so ancient and interesting, so full of remarkable architecture that it would be difficult to ignore. And having begun to unravel its steep cobbled streets, spiralling up through arched gateways crowned with armorial crests, its terraces and plazas, and its thirteenth-century churches, I found I had spent a couple of hours there. Clearly the Road to Santiago possessed an embarrassment of riches and I could not possibly hope to see them all.

The final ten miles to Estella were made without stopping. Resisting temptation, I pedalled past the place near the village of Lorca where Aimery Picaud reported that Navarrese rogues used to encourage passing pilgrims to water their horses. The river was highly contaminated, and horses drinking from it died on the spot, at which the crafty Navarrese, who had been sharpening their knives in preparation, immediately flayed them. Picaud's party lost two animals in this way and he was understandably indignant about it. Several pages of his guide are devoted to informing pilgrims about which Spanish rivers are safe to drink from and which have fish that are poisonous or unwholesome to foreigners. The fact that pollution was a problem in medieval times was something else that made me feel less distant from that age.

I remembered Picaud's assurance that Estella's River Ega was particularly wholesome as I lay sleepless that night in the *refugio*, only feet away, listening to it thundering like a train on its rain-swollen passage, bearing a burden of uprooted trees and other detritus. The day had been sunny and pleasant but the amounts of water that had fallen over the last few weeks was still having its effects upon the rivers of northern Spain, some of which had burst their banks.

The *refugio* at Estella was large and depressing, the first floor of a run-down modern building, lacking both cooking and washing facilities. It was really no more than a place to doss down on dubious mattresses in grimy rooms, and a far cry from the comforts of Cizur Menor. Had I arrived earlier I would probably have decided to look for an hotel, though in retrospect I was glad that I hadn't. Now that I had the opportunity to do so, it seemed important to take the journey as it came, and not to waste time and thought over things which did not matter.

I had only just reached Estella in time to view the extraordinary twisted column in the cloisters of St Peter's church, San Pedro de la Rua, before it was locked up for the night. The other six or seven historic churches were already firmly shut, but Estella was the sort of place where it was very pleasant simply to wander around the old streets. As Aimery Picaud noted it was 'full of all delights'. In his day it had been the seat of the Kings of Navarre, and very French in character (which was doubtless why the xenophobic Picaud had so approved of it). The modest palace with its capital depicting Roland's fight with the giant Ferragut still stands, newly restored, across from the church of St Peter. In 1492 Jewish merchants expelled from

Castile were invited to settle in Estella and a row of their very attractive houses stands further down the same wide street, currently also undergoing restoration.

I discovered a pleasant restaurant for an evening meal, but although it was after nine I was the only diner. This had its advantages, for seeing me struggling with the unfamiliar menu, the waitress had time to take me to the kitchen where I was able to choose a splendid fish (Picaud had also pronounced favourably on Estella's fish). Night had fallen by the time I had finished, and I was more than ready for sleep.

I had collected the key to the *refugio* from the town hall earlier in the evening, together with a stamp for my *Credencial del Peregrino*. Following the directions I had been given, I set off to find my bed, with the full moon lighting my way and reflecting off the swollen river at my side.

I couldn't find the light switch in the dark, rambling building but through the uncurtained windows overlooking the river the moonlight poured in. I chose the smallest room and spread my groundsheet over a bed. There was no way of washing off the day's sweat and dirt except in the dark rushing waters below, which I decided was too dangerous for more than a perfunctory rinsing of hands and face. A wet flannel would have to do for the rest.

It was so cold that I got into my sleeping bag to read 'Compline'. When I finished, I switched off the torch and lay watching the moon sailing among racing clouds which changed from white to bronze as they crossed the bright disc. River, clouds and moon were all of a piece, like a great symphony, echoing the words I had just been reading.

'. . . Brethren, be sober, be vigilant, because your adversary the devil goeth about as a roaring lion, seeking whom he might devour, whom resist steadfast in the faith.'

7

Into the Rioja

From Estella the *Camino* takes a south-westerly course, which brought me directly into the teeth of a strong cold wind. The wide exposed terrain provided no buffer at all to its force; even wearing most of the clothes I had with me – two shirts, shell-emblazoned sweater, windproof jacket, with the waterproof jacket over everything, still I shivered and my eyes watered behind their cycling glasses. But for all it offered little comfort, the landscape was arresting. Bright green fields made a single seamless carpet that rolled on to the foot of a great white falaise to the north. Other diversely painted hills reared up all around sharply drawn under a harsh blue sky splattered with black clouds. The vastness of the view was daunting and the absence of detail made progress seem infinitely slow and laboured. It was the sort of stretch where foot-weary pilgrims might well despair of ever reaching Santiago. For criminals who were sent on the pilgrimage as an alternative to a prison sentence, a practice still followed by Belgium up to the present century, such days must have made them wonder whether a cell would not have been much the easier option.

On a bicycle, energy conserving machine though it

undoubtedly is, it was the sort of day where it would have been infinitely better to have been going in the opposite direction. My efforts appeared to be getting me nowhere. Where the hills rose in my path, the combination of wind and gradient frequently brought me to a complete standstill. Sheer determination is all that keeps one going on these occasions, together with the belief – based on experience, but nonetheless not easy to remember – that it will prove worth it in the end.

In such conditions any excuse to stop is a blessed relief and my first halt at Los Arcos, in the ornate, gold-dripping parish church had the additional advantage of total contrast. The lofty Gothic interior, overlaid with a great mixture of styles was neither restful nor of great architectural distinction, but it was a delight, particularly the exuberant Baroque altars and furnishings which dominated everything else. What I particularly enjoyed were the organ pipes jutting out horizontally like brazen trumpets from high up on either side of the narrow choir. The larger ones had faces on them, with wide square mouths painted around the vents:

'O Lord open thou our lips
And our mouths shall show forth thy praise'

I had to go first to the *padré's* house to get the church opened, and, kind man that he was, he gave me coffee and made me comfortable by his fire while he found his *sello* to stamp my *certificación de paso*. With the aid of my small dictionary and a few words of French and English he told me what a good idea it was to travel to Santiago at this time of year. 'People have time to speak to you,' he said. 'In July it is terrible, so many people, buses, and many, many cars. You cannot get through the street. That is not the time for real pilgrims.' All of which made me feel much better about the cold and the wind and the lack of other pilgrims – an absence that had begun to worry me.

I pushed on towards the next stop, far more concerned about the possibility of an early lunch than about seeing another octagonal chapel at Torres del Rio, for thoughts of food seem to dominate everything on such days. When I arrived at the tiny hamlet and realised there was no likelihood of any refreshment, I could hardly be bothered to climb up the short hill to the church. This would have been a great pity as even from the outside the elegant little structure was worth a longer detour than the hundred yards or so I had to make. The steep village street with its antique houses was not to be despised either, with stout ladies leaning out of windows to scream to one another concerning the whereabouts of Senora Miranda who had the key. Torres del Rio's octagonal church was another Crusader foundation, but unlike Eunate, it was a Templar church and had been built by Moorish architects. A great feeling of space had been achieved within its small compass, largely because of its fine vaulted roof that incorporated a lantern, and it was in fact far more reminiscent of Holy Land architecture than Eunate had been. But lovely though it was it did nothing to assuage my ever-growing hunger, and I had to struggle on for a further seven miles against the bully of a wind, which clearly had no intention of making life easy for me.

'Mangare, mangare?' I asked of the blue-tinged passers-by in the cobbled streets of pretty little Viana, hoping that the Spanish word would be something like; and they, clearly used to all sorts of barbarous utterances from passing stran-gers directed me without any signs of incomprehension to a serious looking café full of workmen busily tucking into platefuls of food. Once installed I could get out my phrase book and ask for the *menú del día*. This produced a large bowl of chickpea stew, another trout with a slice of crisp bacon – the last of this regional speciality as I was on the point of leaving Navarre – and a *crème caramel* all for around the equivalent of five pounds. I did experience a twinge of guilt that I could be made so happy simply by eating. A true pilgrim, surely, should have her mind set on higher things.

Disappointingly there was nothing relevant to medieval pilgrimage remaining in Viana. Its major claim to fame now is as the burial place of the brilliant and unscrupulous Cesare Borgia, the illegitimate son of the dissolute Pope Alexander VI. Cesare Borgia was one of the models Machiavelli drew on heavily for *The Prince*, and like his literary counterpart he suffered no moral scruples about achieving his ambitions. After a breathtaking career of political murders and machinations, he had been killed in a skirmish in 1503, at the age of thirty-two. Had some spiteful cleric not been true to the vengeful spirit of his times and removed the tomb from the church I wouldn't have been able to see it at all for, true to Spanish custom, Viana's churches were firmly shut after midday. But there it was – a large ancient tombstone with the name Cesare Borgia on it set into the pavement for passers-by to walk upon.

From Viana I passed almost immediately into the rich agricultural lands of the Rioja, an autonomous region now, but once much fought over. Latterly it was a valuable part of Castile. When Alfonso VI had wrested it from Navarre in 1076 one of the first things he put his mind to was improving the pilgrim route across it in order to promote trade. Wide rivers watered these plains and one of them, the Río Oja, gave its name to the region. For the bridging of these rivers Alfonso employed the services of two gifted monks, later to become St Dominic and St Juan of Ortega. I crossed the impressive River Ebro on a replica of their first bridge to the bustling capital of Logroño which had sprung up on the west bank as a result of their work.

Logroño was the most modern town I had seen since leaving London. Full of rushing traffic and tall faceless buildings, it could have been almost anywhere. It was rather disorientating until the first yellow arrow led me back to the now familiar time warp where the *Camino* passed through the medieval remnants of Logroño on the ghost of its ancient route, while the traffic of the parallel modern thoroughfare thundered away on the left. The cathedral being closed, there was nothing of sufficient substance to encourage me to linger, though I did pause before the lively statue of St James as *Matamoros* on the wall of the Church of Santiago. Not far from Logroño is the site of the Battle of Clavijo where, in 834, King Ramiro I is said to have decided to fight the Moors rather than to continue to pay them the yearly tribute of a hundred virgins. It was on this battlefield of Clavijo that St James first appeared on his white charger at the head of the Christian army, laying about him with a great sword until he had piled up a personal tally of 70,000 infidels.

Many scholars claim that the battle itself was a myth, with or without the intervention of the saint. What is certain, however, is that real or imaginary, the battle was the basis of what seems like one of the longest running frauds in history. Some three hundred years after St James had put in his first appearance as *Matamoros*, certain clerical dignitaries in the cathedral of Santiago alleged that in thankfulness for the saint's help in the Battle of

Clavijo, King Ramiro I had instituted a corn and wine tax on the Spanish people to be paid in perpetuity into the cathedral coffers. A document ordering this tax, the Diploma of Ramiro I, was alleged to be held in the cathedral archives, and on the basis of it monarchs were encouraged to make shift to collect the tax from their subjects. Many attempts were made to force the authorities to produce this Ramiro Diploma, and when, finally, no further prevarication was possible, the cathedral authorities were forced to plead that the original document had gone missing. Only an allegedly faithful twelfth-century copy was available and this fooled no one. Few people concerned can have doubted for a moment that the whole affair was a fraud cooked up by the cathedral authorities in order to pay for the cost of building their magnificent church. Nonetheless it was not until 1834, exactly one thousand years after the debated battle, that the tax was finally abolished.

While I was looking at the saint on his dashing charger and wondering how he would have viewed the crooked tax exacted in his name, I was hailed by an old man. He turned out to be a local pilgrim who had been to Santiago four times on foot and who was eager to tell me about it. He looked set to be another Ancient Mariner had not the lack of a common language prevented him going into details. As it was, it made a pleasant meeting; I awakened his memories of the pilgrimage, while for me it was another reminder that I wasn't making an isolated journey, solitary though it might seem for much of the time.

The low arched gate by which I left Logroño was the prettiest thing I had seen there. It was also like Alice's Looking Glass; once through it and I was back abruptly into the twentieth century, trying not to be intimidated on the death-defying road to Navarette. Six miles of purgatory followed, during which I tried not to nurse uncharitable thoughts about the speeding drivers. And then the day's struggle was over, as I reached Navarette and settled into the peace and quiet of the *refugio* in the grounds of the *Seminario* of the *Padres Camilos*.

There was nothing particular about the small town of Navarette except its atmosphere of being left behind with its memories of ancient battles and great events. But again, side by side with the modern road, and only a short distance from it, I was back in familiar territory. Scraps of finer masonry had been incorporated here and there into more modern walls and thresholds, and the lovely Romanesque portal of San Sepulcro, the hospice of the Knights Hospitallers, had been rebuilt as the entrance to the town's cemetery – sparse mementoes for a town that was more important than Logroño in its day, and yet enough to retain the aura of the *Camino Francés*, which by now was unmistakable.

To celebrate the safe ending of another day's journey I bought a bottle of white Rioja wine at the small store. A patient, motherly woman leant her bulk comfortably on her forearms at the counter and watched while I shopped. She corrected my Spanish, naming each item very slowly and clearly after I had mispronounced it from my dictionary and waiting for me to repeat the words correctly after her. It was like being back in the kindergarten class, a nice warm feeling of comfort and security.

Returning to the *refugio* I found that two more pilgrims had arrived; Kurt, a retired doctor from Bavaria, and Theo, a twenty-two-year-old engineering student from Eindhoven in the Netherlands. Theo, like me, was travelling by bicycle and Kurt was walking the route from Arles. All three of us expressed delight at finding fellow pilgrims, and since we were all going to eat at the *refugio*, we decided to pool our provisions and have a civilised meal together. There was no dining room or kitchen, just two small dormitories and a cold-water-only bathroom, but by pushing beds around a little, we rigged a table and seating and spread out a simple meal of bread and cheese, fruit and salad and the Rioja. In fact we had two bottles of wine as Theo had bought one too, which certainly helped in the time-honoured pilgrim tradition of sharing our stories. We talked far into the night and when we had parted the following morning I found I knew more about them than I did about acquaintances I'd known for years. There is a freedom in talking to people you are unlikely to meet again.

Theo was a tall strong young man who had cycled at least four hundred miles further than I had, and in about half the time. He wasn't really interested in old churches and things like that he said, so he did not stop much. He was making the pilgrimage because he had read about it in a travel magazine, and had thought it was something he would like to try. It was a challenge. He was fed up with his course and wasn't sure any more if engineering was really what he wanted to do. He hoped the journey would give him time to think things out, but even if he found no answers, he thought the experience would have been worth it. Even being alone was something new to him, and it had felt very strange. Several times he had been on the point of giving up and going home. But after a week all that had changed and now he was really enjoying himself. He was looking forward to arriving at Santiago and wanted to push on as fast as he could.

Kurt said he didn't mind when he arrived. Walking the *Camino* was easy in spite of blisters, wet feet, aching shoulders and the like. Life was reduced to its basics: eating, sleeping and walking. It left your mind free. There was an unmistakable air about Kurt that I came to recognise as the 'pilgrim look'. People encountered in remote mountains or on desert crossings sometimes have it too. It comes, I think, from being alone with one's thoughts for long periods, while one's body is being disciplined by long hard activity. Possibly the 'pilgrim look' reflects something of the inner struggle, or maybe it reveals a new sense of purpose or awareness, but however one interprets it, it is a less guarded expression than people usually present to the world.

I found Kurt's story particularly interesting. He was the only son of a man who had abandoned the priesthood in order to marry – a rather scandalous thing to do sixty years ago. Kurt said he thought his father had remained a priest in his heart and was never really happy or at peace with himself. He had died quite young, and Kurt had long intended to make the pilgrimage to Santiago as a sort of memorial to him. It was a journey his father had wanted to make, but had felt debarred from.

By comparison with his father's, Kurt's own life had been very straightforward. He had pursued a successful career in medicine, had married someone he had known since childhood, and had raised four healthy children, who were now all happily married themselves. It was the death of his wife the year before, coinciding with his retirement, that had given him the jolt he needed to finally fulfil the debt he felt he owed his father. 'If I left it,' he said, 'I realised I would never have the courage to do it. But you only have to start, the rest follows by itself.'

Being with Kurt and Theo for an evening made me think how nice it would be to make the journey with other people. The ideal I felt, would be to walk or cycle alone all day, and meet up in the evening to share a meal, talk over the events of the day, and continue the issues that had been raised the previous evenings. But any ideas we three had discussed, or new thoughts we had raised would have to be pursued alone.

One thing all three of us had agreed upon was how right it felt to be staying in the *refugios* whose simple basic accommodation was so much more in keeping with the spirit of the *Camino* than hotels would have been. Only when there was no hot water with which to wash, or when all one's clothes were wringing wet and there was nowhere to dry them did one hanker for greater comfort.

The following morning dawned even more darkly than the previous one and I was glad I had only a short day planned. Theo would be miles ahead of me by noon and Kurt would be somewhat behind, so there was little prospect of us meeting up again. Accordingly we made our farewells all, I think, feeling a little richer for the evening's company.

My journal records the day as one of 'steep hills, monumental rain, and severe cold'. Further down the same page is another heartfelt moan of 'wind like a cold fist in the face, biting rain, freezing fingers, with racing trucks, cars and more hills making the whole thing a most one-sided battle'. A line of Bunyan, followed immediately by a question mark shows how low I was at that point.

'. . . There's no discouragement shall make him once relent his first avowed intent to be a pilgrim'?

In between the two *crises de coeur* is the record of a visit to the monastery of Santa María la Real at Nájera. I think it was the only time in the day when the icy rain running down inside my collar ceased to matter. The church contains the ancient royal pantheon of the Kings of Navarre, for Nájera was once their capital before it was annexed by Castile. The sense of the *Camino* is very strong in the small area around the centre of the old town where the river flows in a great bow close to the overhanging cliff that shelters the church. The present structure is sixteenth century, extensively restored in recent times, but the ancient battered tombs of the kings, illuminated by a suitable greenish light, rest in a grotto beneath the choir carved out of the rock of the cliffs. In a side chapel is the later twelfth-century tomb of Queen Doña Blanca of Pamplona who died giving birth to a future King of Castile. It is one of the most beautifully carved tombs I have seen outside of Greece. Most of it is biblical scenes, but one panel shows Doña Blanca's soul slipping from her body in the form of a little child. The tombs were only a part of the charm of the place, however. The whole building had an unusual quality of space and harmony that I hadn't encountered so far on the journey. Possibly this was because it was in the care of the Franciscans and reflected something of their founder's simplicity.

Between Najera and Santo Domingo de la Calzada is one of the stretches that will draw me back to repeat the pilgrimage one day. For I saw none of its attractions, nor did I make any of the traditional diversions to interesting tombs, villages and monasteries off the route. It was possible only to battle on head down and concentrate on turning the pedals.

My reward for perseverance was to finish the day at the most comfortable *refugio* of the route, where the sybaritic delight of a hot shower did much to restore my flagging spirits. Santo Domingo de la Calzada is the sainted bridge-builder's own town; the place where he had his hermit's cell and where in 1109 he finally died. The bridge he built is still in place across the river and his tomb is in the cathedral that stands at the head of the pilgrim's way, with its lofty tower visible from afar. All of which makes him seem very much a real person, something I don't necessarily feel about all saints, especially some of the more obscure ones.

Of course, had Santo Domingo been merely an inspired builder of roads, bridges, pilgrim hospices and churches, the matter would have ended with his death. Sainthood requires miracles and on that score Santo Domingo acquits himself satisfactorily. But the most famous miracle connected with the town is sometimes ascribed to the intervention of St James himself. Who ever gets the final credit for it, however, the miracle known as the 'pendu dépendu' (the hanged man unhanged) is still celebrated in quite the most bizarre fashion.

The story concerns an aged couple and their teenage son who are passing through Santo Domingo on their way to Santiago. The son is wrongly accused of theft by a servant girl whose advances he rejects. After the young man has been wrongfully hanged for the offence, the sorrowing parents continue to Santiago where they make their offerings at the shrine. On the return journey, when they are again in Santo Domingo, they cast their eyes up to the gibbet where their son is hanging, and to their amazement he speaks to them. St James has intervened on his behalf and restored him to life (or St Domingo has kept him alive because of his innocence). Whichever was the case, the stunned parents run straight round to the magistrate who ordered the execution to inform him of the startling new facts of the case. He is at his dinner at the time, a fat hen and a capon nicely roasted before him, and he replies sarcastically that if the boy is still alive after all this time then so are these fowls which he is about to eat. At which point the cock and hen both leap up from the platter (fully fledged again presumably) and set up a great crowing and cackling.

The lovely interior of the cathedral of Santo Domingo de la Calzada is full of treasures, not least the saint's exquisite late Gothic tomb. And high on a wall quite close to it is probably the most ornate hen coop ever occupied by a very live pair of white domestic fowl. They are said to be descendants of those same roast fowls that had so miraculous a resurrection, and their feathers are sought after with the same fervour that our ancestors once collected the relics of saints. But somehow they do not portray the same feeling of reality as St Domingo himself, and as for the raucous *cock a doodle doo* that echoes through the church, even at such moments as the elevation of the host, I think that requires more powers of disassociation than I possess. I was, however, pleased to learn that the birds were not condemned to a life sentence in their gilded cage, but served only a six-week term before being relieved by another team.

8

The Lands of Old Castile

I rode out of the Rioja on a crisp blue day of rare calm. Although the sun shone, giving the illusion of warmth, my fingers ached and tingled with the cold and my breath hung in the sparkling air. The way led straight as an arrow over a broad green undulating plain with a scattering of brown trees just coming into leaf – early spring again – my third experience of it in a single year. It was as if time had forgotten to move on. Then suddenly above the green plains I saw the towering white outlines of the mountains of the Sierra de la Demanda. The stark snow-covered peaks transformed the landscape instantly. It no longer seemed strange to be feeling cold on so bright a day. The sense of coming into more exotic lands than I had seen so far on the journey quickened the pulse, and the idea of time standing still faded.

It was a suitably impressive entry into the lands of Old Castile, the heartland of Spain, whose name reflects the great number of castles that were built there over the centuries in the long fight against the Moorish forces of Islam. And what a day to see it for the first time! From conditions of head down against the wind, grit the teeth and bear it, once more I had an embarrassment of riches. When the sun had taken the edge off the early morning chill it was pure bliss to be on a bicycle. I could have pushed on hour after hour, enjoying every turn of the pedals. Was this what the Roncesvalles questionnaire had meant by 'sport' as a motive for the pilgrimage, I wondered? If so then I would tick it twice over, for it is at times like these that I feel closest to God. Like the writer of the Psalms rejoicing in the wonder of creation and in man's place in it, I too feel a great sense of awe and delight in the thought of 'I am fearfully and wonderfully made'.

But I could not give in completely to the sheer exhilaration of movement, for there was a continuous stream of things to stop and admire. There were villages to make detours to in order to view a particularly interesting font, or a line of old cottages, or a wayside cross – of which, not unnaturally, there were a great number on the *Camino*, and many of them quite lovely. Pausing by the roadside to enjoy the views more closely was also necessary, as the landscape continued to reveal fresh, arresting facets of itself.

This was more like being on holiday than on a pilgrimage I thought, and immediately wondered what I meant by that. Was it wrong to be enjoying myself? Were pilgrims supposed to be miserable? I certainly hadn't set out in the belief that pilgrimage needed to be a penitential journey, but by this stage in the journey I had studied a great many Last Judgements carved on the walls of medieval churches and I was satiated with depictions of hell and with all the ingenious and hideous tortures that the fertile medieval mind could dream up as the wages of sin. As a result, I had fallen into the trap of thinking that all serious pilgrims must be deeply troubled by the state of their souls and earnestly intent on expiating their sins before it was too late. The last few days of slogging onward against wind and rain had done little to dislodge that idea.

John Bunyan has also been much in my mind because of his ubiquitous hymn 'He Who Would Valiant Be', and Bunyan's pilgrim is certainly no model of jollity. I suppose writing his *Pilgrim's Progress* in prison probably would give an author a rather jaundiced view of life. Certainly there is nowhere in Christian's progress towards the Celestial City where you could say he was possessed of the sort of joy reflected in the Psalms. And then the Celestial City itself also presents a problem. Call it the New Jerusalem, heaven, Paradise, or what you will, it still comes over as a rather boring place. Who, other than a dedicated musician would feel happy at the prospect of strumming on a harp all day? Or 'Praising the Lamb without Ceasing'? Of course I realise that it is a problem of language struggling to express the inexpressible, and most Christians interpret these words and images in their own way and presumably have differing ideas about what it all means. But hell is illustrated by examples from everyday life that are easy to relate to and it would, I think, help considerably to have similar ways of enhancing the image of heaven.

The only writer I know who begins to quicken the imagination in regard to the after life in general, and heaven in particular, is C.S. Lewis in his Narnia books. The final one of the series, *The Last Battle*, tackles many of Christianity's knottier theological problems, particularly those dealing with death, Judgement and the Hereafter. Because it was written for children, he could not fudge the issues, and while being gripping stuff as all good children's literature must be, its simplicity is also profound and scholarly, and much admired by many eminent theologians. I particularly love his image of the Resurrection Body's delight – running and leaping through an idyllic countryside without ever becoming tired. He uses this image to mirror a glimpse into the joys of heaven – a sense of joy, which does indeed echo the Psalms.

If joy is indeed part of the awareness of God, as both the psalmist and C.S. Lewis believed, then this day's ride was a particularly blessed stage of my journey. The feeling of an all-embracing happiness was so sustained that I began to wonder if some special influence was at work on the *Camino* hereabouts – Santo Domingo, the builder of the road, perhaps, since his tomb was so close, and since he had been so keen to help pilgrims. A visit to the *Bar León*, where a special pilgrim log is kept, did nothing to dispel the fancy. Reading through the entries that went back several years, it was clear that I was not the only person to find this an inspirational stretch of the Santiago Road. Many entries were what I would normally describe as way over the top; all about being 'accompanied by angels' and the like. I could only read the ones in English, French or Dutch, so what was written in the tongues of less inhibited races I could only imagine. In complete contrast to the more flowery entries, however, was an English one, the work of someone who had clearly not been having a wonderful day. He had also been brooding on the story of the hanged man unhanged ever since leaving Santo Domingo de la Calzada. A blank page of the log had been a spur to his thoughts, which had erupted in an impassioned, blow by blow, account of the miracle. He seemed to have believed in it all implicitly. Yet at the end, missing the point entirely, he had written 'Bloody Spanish! just the sort of thing some of them would do, hang a pilgrim!' Xenophobia strikes many travellers from time to time; I could only hope S.G. of Blandford had opportunities to sample the kindness of the Spanish also. His entry was followed by a splendidly succinct one in a child's round hand. 'Kes 9 years, a pilgrim'. And if one didn't fall in love with the human race there and then, after sharing all these outpourings, I decided there could be little hope at all for one in this life.

By noon the day was golden. The wind had sprung up again, but it had swung a hundred and eighty degrees from its usual quarter and was now directly behind me, a rare 'Sabbath Wind' which Isbil Roncal had called 'St James pushing on the pilgrims'. All I had to do for much of the time was to sit up and let the wind do the work – cycle sailing! I was flying over the hills with an ease I thought I had long lost, together with my youth. Had I not had my mind set on nearer sights, I felt as if I could have pushed on and on into the ever-receding blue distance. But I had planned to spend the night at a *refugio* in an ancient primitive monastery, a little way before Burgos and some distance from the road. Accordingly I exchanged the pleasures of broad smooth tarmac and effortless speed for bumpy narrow country lanes and tracks, and found the sudden quiet and the different smells, sounds and sights an even greater joy. The last few kilometres were on the walkers' track and this eventually brought me to a clearing in the forests of Montes de Oca where I found the lovely cluster of buildings begun by San Juan de Ortega, the disciple and co-worker of Santo Domingo.

The buildings were in the process of restoration, which is to say that extensive work had been carried out and then abandoned before it was quite finished. Lack of funds accounted for many such arrested schemes in Spain, a common problem in countries with an abundant architectural heritage combined with limited funds. Out of sight at the back of the monastery, a dismantled crane, rails, and other building machinery had been left to rust and crumble beneath the long grass of what had once been cloisters. The romantic dilapidation that was exposed to public view had been arrested and stabilised, but not entirely dispelled – an admirable Spanish compromise. The complex of church, shrine and priest's house presented a serene spectacle in the late afternoon, with the light falling obliquely across the fine west façade of the monastery church.

Don José María Alonso was the priest in sole charge of this beautiful place, and apart from him it was quite deserted. When I arrived he was sitting in his car, listening to a football commentary on the radio, the excited chatter an incongruous intrusion in the stillness. Like his sainted twelfth-century predecessor, Don José was a friend of pilgrims and devoted to their welfare. He insisted on leaving his football to welcome me and make me coffee. He would have prepared a full-scale meal had I not protested that I had eaten a large lunch only an hour or so before and could manage nothing else. Only when he had shown me the pilgrim quarters and made sure I had everything I needed did he return to his football match, and was soon once more deeply engrossed.

After paying my respects at the saint's fine tomb and exploring the other buildings, I spent most of the remaining hours of daylight sitting on a bench in a sheltered spot outside, enjoying the sun and writing up my journal. As it was Sunday, and I had not found a church service to attend, I also read through the 'Office of None' in the monastery church. Parts of this lovely church were as San Juan had built it, a testament to his great skill as an architect. The long and thoughtful Psalm 119 which formed the bulk of the 'Office of None' seemed an appropriate reading and something with which San Juan himself would have been familiar. Whether it was reading it aloud there, or whether the joy of the day itself made me see everything with new eyes, I don't know, but the psalm struck me with a new force of meaning I had not seen in it before. Being all about the keeping of laws and commandments it had never been a favourite of mine. I associated it with a horrible part of my childhood when, because of the war, I had been evacuated to a particularly narrow and bigoted non-conformist household. In an atmosphere of dark ignorance I suffered several years of the most miserable Sabbaths imaginable (I still cannot say the word Sabbath without a shudder). Forced to sit inactive and desperately bored for hour after hour, without even the solace of a book simply because it was the 'Lord's Day' was a dreadful experience. The sense of imprisonment was bad enough for a six-year-old child, but the implanting of the image of a 'vengeful and judgemental God who required his creatures to be miserable' was the greater and more insidious evil. How I even partially recovered from this early warping could only, I think, have been through an act of grace.

But this day in the lovely setting of San Juan's church I was able to read through Psalm 119 as though for the first time, and I saw that in fact it was all about freedom, not coercion, a response of the heart. The whole psalm in fact seemed to be about approaching God and his commandments through joy; the complete reverse of what my oppressive guardians had attempted to instil in me.

There was also a short sentence from Galatians in this 'Office of None' which echoes the tone of the Psalm 119, but strikes home more immediately.

> 'Bear ye one another's burdens, and so fulfil
> the law of Christ.'

I sat on for a while, wondering just how solitary travellers could bear one another's burdens. Thinking about what I had read in the log book of the *Bar León* and in the *refugios*, it seemed to me that, although not face-to-face encounters, people did relate to one another through this sharing of their thoughts, and sometimes quite powerfully. Slowly I had become aware, not only of people making the journey today, but of a great network of people past and present, all travelling the *Camino*. The log books were a constant reminder that I was not making the journey alone. From there it was a only a step to having these people in mind and a part of daily prayer.

A pilgrim I was particularly aware of at this time was a young woman named Tamsin Hooper whose entries I had come across several times. She had passed this way in early February, and because she was walking I hoped I might catch up with her before Santiago. I never did but she was a real companion of the way. Her short forthright entries had taken on a more emotional tone in this monastery. She had arrived in the dark after a hard cold day. Night had fallen as she was still plodding through the forest. She had nothing to eat and was just resigning herself to a lonely hungry night in her tent when the dim lights of St Juan de Ortega had suddenly opened up before her. After being fed and pampered by Don José her sense of thankfulness sang out of the page.

Don José, his football match over, called me into his wildly untidy kitchen. 'No woman to care for me,' he joked, pushing a few things aside to make space at the wide cluttered table. This was one of the occasions I most regretted my lack of Spanish, for it was evident that Don José possessed a keen sense of humour, as well as having a wealth of information to impart. Even with our minimal communication he had managed to tease me unmercifully about travelling by bike, claiming that it was not a real pilgrimage unless done on foot. And actually, judging by the bits of the walkers' route I had managed to ride, I couldn't altogether disagree with him. With so much of the *Camino* under the tarmac of a busy main road, it felt more in keeping with the spirit of medieval pilgrimage to take the alternative routes right away from traffic. An ideal solution, I thought, would be to upgrade these tracks to make them suitable for cyclists. But Don José had been talking about something more subtle than enjoyment or evocation of the past. It was the inner experience of pilgrimage that he felt was easier to come by on foot, particularly for the young who were his special care. He admitted, however, with a rare note of seriousness, that some people could walk the whole way to Santiago without ever knowing the meaning of pilgrimage, while others could be true pilgrims even travelling there by bus. It was all 'in the heart'. There was something about pilgrims, he said, that he had come to love: they were 'the salt of the earth'.

It transpired that apart from the relics of San Juan de Ortega in his splendid sarcophagus on the other side of the wall, and the spirit of the Jeronymite monks who had lived here for four hundred years (and the camaraderie of my invisible army of pilgrims), I was to spend the night alone in the monastery. Don José is not a young man and he finds the chilly altitude of San Juan de Ortega far too severe until somewhere near the end of June. Until then he returns each night to Burgos down on the plains. Before he left he made me a supper of eggs deliciously fried in olive oil, followed by yoghurt and fruit, with a glass of his rough red wine as a barrier against the cold. After this I was escorted into the monastery and instructed on how to lock myself and Roberts securely in there for the night.

'Brethren, be sober, be vigilant.'

He was right about the cold. As I climbed the stairs to the dormitories the chill seemed to seep out from the walls. It is a fifteenth-century, two-storey structure built around a small central well, with a narrow balcony running around the upper floor, a completely utilitarian building making no concessions at all to weakness or comfort. The dormitories are bare-floored and furnished only with black iron bunks. But if the recent restoration had done nothing to dispel the primitive simplicity of the place, neither had it robbed it of its essential character. It was indescribably peaceful and again there was that indefinable sense of rightness about it. Not for a moment did I wish myself anywhere else, even for the sake of a hot bath. I went to bed wearing silk long johns, cycling tights, socks, silk vest and sweater, and piled blankets over and under my sleeping bag. Had I brought a woolly hat I would have worn that too. It was ridiculous really, lying there bundled up against the cold, my nose freezing, and yet hugging the knowledge of how privileged I was to be there, and conscious of the same warm happiness I had felt the entire day.

The long freewheel down from the Montes de Oca started well on another cold sunny morning, but it became progressively less pleasant as I hit the spreading outskirts of Burgos, the city of El Cid, frenetic with its Monday morning traffic. I had been looking forward to Burgos as one of the highlights of the pilgrimage, but only when I reached the ornate stone bridge opposite the splendid Puerta de Santa

María did I feel able to relax for a moment from the battle for personal survival and examine my surroundings. The exuberant froth of stone ornamentation across the Arlanzón River was no bad way to take a first long look at Burgos, a city whose buildings certainly appeared to be in keeping with its reputation.

Burgos had been the first capital of Old Castile, the centre of the Reconquest and of vital importance to the Santiago pilgrimage. Its influence had waned gradually with the Christian advance southwards, until in 1492 it lost its place to Valladolid, which became the unified Spain's new capital. But with the considerable wealth from its wide fertile plains, Burgos had continued to thrive and to embellish its monuments, and the pilgrimage had continued to flow through it with its attendant trade. Unlike Logroño, modernity had not eclipsed Burgos. From where I stood I could see a fine substantial pilgrim city rising above the splendid gateway.

If I wanted to enter the city by the traditional pilgrim route, however, I could not go in through this sixteenth-century gate of Puerta de Santa María, but needed to retrace my way westward to the smaller medieval gate of San Juan. I was glad I did this, for nowhere on the route are there more architectural treasures of various periods of the pilgrimage than along this half-mile of the old city of Burgos, and the maze of ancient streets that have been allowed to remain unwidened added greatly to the pleasure.

At the end of this half-mile stands the wonderfully spired and pinnacled cathedral. My guide book waxed lyrical about this church, claiming that it showed the true genius of Spanish architecture. But possibly I had seen far too much excellent architecture already for one day and should have spent more time there. For although I too fell for the fairy-tale charm of Burgos's 'Queen of Gothic Cathedrals', I also found it difficult to take seriously. Nowhere, outside of Germany and Austria, and perhaps not even there, had I seen a building quite so magnificently overdone. It is the result of many rebuildings and embellishments in which each successive architect seems to have striven to outdo his predecessor. The outcome is a greater wealth of spires, finials, crockets, buttresses and stone lacework than I would have believed possible in a single building. 'Marvellous stonework,' my journal notes, 'but somehow the total effect doesn't inspire as churches do which rely more on a total harmony – like Salisbury, Chartres or Durham.'

The centre point of the interior of Burgos Cathedral is the vast stone lantern of tremendous grace and ingenuity, but it is difficult to see properly because a visitor can no longer stand directly beneath it. The underlying genius of the original Gothic structure has been destroyed by a large, totally enclosed and slab-like choir which takes up most of the nave and intrudes into the crossing. The sense of space, the long perspectives and the harmony of line have been totally eclipsed by this intrusion. It is a wonderfully rich place, but it feels more like a major museum of religious art than a living church, and it made me eager to return to the reality and freedom of the *Camino*.

Outside again in the sunshine I was about to unchain Roberts from the railings when a man with a bundle of guide books in his hand approached. 'Don't leave your bicycle here,' he warned. 'There are many thieves about. I will look after it for you, while you visit the cathedral.' I was trying to explain that I had a lock and was quite all right, when an American voice cut in, 'Don't you give him anything, he's a crook', and an argument broke out around me about the price of a guide book he was selling. I hurriedly stowed away the lock and retreated.

While I had been visiting the cathedral, several coach loads of visitors had arrived and there were now people milling thickly about the square in front of the cathedral, their large brash vehicles providing incongruous additions to the scene. This was my first encounter on the journey with tourism on any scale, and as a Londoner, well used to constant influxes of foreign visitors, I was surprised to find how strange it seemed after just a few weeks on the *Camino*. It was as though I had begun to identify with another and earlier time. I found it even more bizarre when people wanted to photograph me with Roberts, making sure they got the scallop shells well to the fore. The result would probably be captioned 'An English Pilgrim in Burgos'. My sense of privacy felt seriously invaded, and I had quickly to remind myself that this too was a part of the pilgrimage. If people wanted to snap a colourful oddity as a memento of their visit to a town on the European Heritage Trail, why should I object? It did me no harm and it might inspire them, if not to go on pilgrimage then perhaps to try bicycling as a way of getting about.

Another American woman, practising charity, thrust a tourist brochure of Burgos into my hand, saying 'Here honey, we've finished with this, save yourself a few pesetas.' As I had arrived a good two hours before the tourist influx and had seen almost everything I wanted to in Burgos, I was soon able to ride away from all this embarrassing attention.

Out in the western suburbs of Burgos I thought I would probably encounter another large crowd visiting the convent of Las Huelgas Reales, the second most famous attraction of Burgos. A Cistercian institution, it

was founded in 1187 by Alfonso VII and his English wife
Eleanor, daughter of Henry II, with the dual purpose of
being a convent for nuns of royal and aristocratic lineage
and a royal pantheon where kings could also be knighted.
The place had expanded over the centuries like so many of
the ancient buildings of Burgos and was now a pot-pourri of
many styles. I particularly wanted to see the small Moorish
chapel of Santiago, where a thirteenth-century statue of St
James had a moveable sword arm, the purpose of which was
to enable kings to be knighted by the saint, rather than by
someone inferior in rank.

There were no crowds or coaches around Las Huelgas
Reales as it happened, because it was closed for the day. I
had to make do with a circuit around the outside perimeter,
and as a small consolation the *Guardia Civil* protecting the
place stamped my *certificación de paso*, so at least I have
a record of the convent's coat of arms. A more solid
consolation was an excellent *menú del día* in a trucker's
restaurant in the western outskirts of the city – fish soup,
a good large steak, ice-cream and coffee, all for just under
six pounds.

Quite close to the restaurant I found what is probably the
most evocative of all Burgos's monuments to the *Camino* –
the medieval Hospital del Rey which had functioned as a
pilgrim's hospice for six hundred and forty years, until it
was very badly damaged by fire in 1835. I was able to see
something of it only because the workmen who had begun
the huge task of restoring the building had left the entrance
to the site open while they went off to lunch. The courtyard
was in a ruinous state, but the portico of the church had
been restored with its ornamentation of scallop shells and
Santiago Matomoros at full stretch above. Of the original
Gothic structure only the western entrance remains and

122

this is known as the Pilgrims' Portal – probably because the way to Santiago lies to the west. One of the masterly Renaissance wooden carvings on the door shows a small band of pilgrims walking the *Camino*. There is a family group among them, including a mother with a babe in arms and a young boy about the age of Kes. With them is what seems like a truly penitential ascetic pilgrim, barefoot and naked except for a loincloth. He seems to have a touch of sainthood about him already as he leans on his stout stick, his steady gaze fixed heavenward. Details of the clothing and footwear of the other pilgrims are faithfully reproduced, with staffs, gourds, scrips and shells much in evidence. It was a fascinating thing to come across and a most appropriate place to take to the road once more.

9

The Wide and Arid Plains

I rode out of Burgos into an ever-widening plain. The sky above it was brilliantly blue and studded with bright, mackerel-coloured clouds. St James was still pushing me on from behind, and to be back on the *Camino Francés* again after the swirl and bustle of the town was like rejoining an old and much-loved friend. The next few days promised to be particularly rewarding, for the route would take me away from the N120, which had been the main thread of the journey since Logroño, and onto small country lanes where it would be rare to encounter a car at all. To travel the old narrow arteries of a country which modern road systems have relegated into byways always gives the illusion of having strayed back into an earlier century. On the *Camino*, with so many tangible remnants of its long and particular history, the illusion is even stronger. The band of pilgrims on the door of the Hospital del Rey, with their staffs and broad-brimmed hats, their stout footwear, scrips and gourds would seem far less out of place on these ancient highways than would I on Roberts.

At Olmillos, where I parted from the N120, there was an arresting semi-ruined castle, possibly a Templar stronghold.

I did not have the opportunity to study it in any detail because as soon as I stopped a rough-looking man, very much the worse for drink, came up and seized hold of Roberts' handlebars. He was probably quite harmless and, as far as I could make out, he only wanted me to accompany him to the nearby bar, but he had so little control of his legs and was lurching about so much that he nearly had us all over in a heap on the road. Extricating myself and Roberts from his grasp was no easy matter and, having seized my moment, I slipped off down a narrow lane, leaving the castle and the interesting little village unexplored.

The broad plain was out of sight to the north, and my way now led across an open *meseta*, a bleak, parched land, where the thin fields showed the unremitting back-breaking toil of centuries. Mounds of stones picked from the earth were dotted about everywhere, but had never been used to build walls or windbreaks. A shepherd moved slowly across a wide sweep of the hillside, calling to his flock of earth-coloured sheep as he went, cajoling and scolding them continuously in a high-pitched voice. I could have imagined myself back in the vast spaces of Asia, for under the wide bright skies with the doleful clanking of the sheep bells the scene had an air of desolate grandeur.

Walkers frequently complained of this particular stretch being monotonous and interminable, but at the pace of the bicycle there was enough change and detail to hold the interest, and I found it one of the strangest and most satisfying sections of the journey. The ancient stone crosses that marked each small crossroads, a small valley where a life-giving spring had created a green oasis, the scattered ruins of lonely farms and an occasional village – a single street of squat top-heavy stone-built houses – all assumed a heightened importance in the wild barrenness of the landscape.

Nearer to Hontanas, where I was planning to spend the night, the land grew a touch more gracious. Hontanas means fountains, and clearly water was the key to settlements in this dry land. The small fields and gardens around the village seemed almost lush in comparison with the open *meseta*. Hontanas itself was impressive and more like a real pilgrim village than anything I had yet seen. A church of enormous proportions dominated the twenty or thirty houses built of rough stone, wattle and daub which clustered around it. The narrow winding streets, havens against the biting winds of the *meseta* and the intense heat of summer, were warm now, yellow in the afternoon sun and redolent of byres and baking bread. The charm of the old dwellings was not seriously marred by the addition of the occasional modern aluminium window frame, but more than half the houses were empty and in varying stages of decay. There had been a serious leaching of the population to the city over the past few years, as has happened in rural areas all over Europe.

The *refugio* was at the top of the small newly restored town hall – OPERA VINCIT 1765. The room was low-ceilinged, with a shuttered window a foot square, set just beneath the beetling eaves. It contained six bunk beds cheek-by-jowl, with barely space enough to pass between them. A tiny room across the landing housed a lavatory and a wash basin with a single cold tap. I thought it would have proved a difficult place in which to practise true Christian charity had it been full, but once again I would be spending the night alone.

I had not had a proper wash in days and, unlike a medieval pilgrim, the need for cleanliness had been bred into me as an essential of decent living. Unless I removed the invisible layer of sweat which clogged my pores I not only felt uncomfortable, I also suffered the dismal guilt of having failed in my duty. Nevertheless, it took no small degree of will power to wash even essential parts in the ice-cold water of Hontanas. I tried to concentrate on thoughts of the Celtic monks of old, standing all night long up to their chests in the freezing seas off the coasts of Scotland and northern England, while they recited the Psalms. But even with this encouraging example my efforts produced no elevation of the spirit to accompany the mortification of the flesh. I was just relieved to get it over.

Cold had been the worst single hardship I had endured on the journey so far. In spite of the bright skies, it had remained decidedly chilly, and in true Spanish style, it always seemed to be far colder indoors than out. Not expecting such low temperatures, I had brought inadequate clothing – no woollens or thermals. I was more or less all right cycling because the exercise kept me warm, except on long downhill stretches. My fingerless riding gloves, however, were totally inadequate, and my hands were usually frozen, as were my ears. I would have bought another pair of gloves and a woolly hat had I been able to find any suitable ones, but such things had proved impossible to come by so far, and I could only hope that I might be able to buy some in Léon before I reached the mountains. To protect my eyes and stop them streaming with water in the wind, I wore my peaked beret pulled well forward over my goggles. This made the beret look like a peaked cap, and in spite of the silver scallop shell badge on the front, some people mistook me for a man.

But the worst effect of the cold was felt in the evenings. After the demands made upon it by strenuous exercise, the body cools down rapidly, and washing in ice-cold water reduces its temperature still further. My solution

was to pile on all the clothes I had and sit swathed in my
sleeping bag while I wrote or read, blowing life back into my
freezing fingertips from time to time. This was very much
in keeping with the medieval period, when it had always
been the custom in northern climes to don extra layers of
clothing on entering the dank castles and draughty halls.
Cold water didn't make laundering easy either. The only
items I bothered with usually were underwear; pinned to the
panniers the next day these dried quickly in the wind. Once
a week I made a real effort to wash shirts and socks.

Temperature aside, Hontanas proved a happy choice of
lodgings. Clean and sanctified I went out to take photographs of the village before the light went. One advantage
of this cold weather was the marvellous light and cloud
effects, and nowhere were these more magnificent than
the evening I spent in this pilgrim village. The mackerel
clouds had darkened a shade to absolute perfection, and
the grey church and houses against the darkly luminous sky
seemed tremendously beautiful and tragic at the same time,
reflecting as they did what was temporal and passing against
what was eternal. 'The sad hour of Compline' was the phrase
that came to mind again as I composed my photographs,
just as it had the evening at La Réole overlooking the river
and watching the people taking their evening stroll. The
feeling was more intense here, the effect no doubt of the
ride through the harsh implacable landscape which made
the human condition seem more fragile than ever.

Doña Anna, who kept the key of the *refugio* and lived
a few doors away from it, had agreed to cook my supper
that evening. She knew a little French, having learnt it
with great difficulty, she said, while working in a clinic in
France before her marriage. The suburban interior of her
house was a strange contrast to the ancient structure, but

it was warm and cheerful which was far more important. Anna made me a *tortilla* – very solid and satisfying – and with some locally produced sweet red wine to go with it, and basking in the warmth of the fire, the last threads of melancholy disappeared. Her thirteen-year-old daughter, Consuela, kept me company while I ate, trying out the flat English phrases she was currently learning at school in Burgos. Anna was very proud of the child and eager to hear her skills praised. She considered education was very important, for there was no future for children in the village. Most of them had to make their living away from home. If Consuela did well, she could maybe find work in Burgos and travel in every day like her father who was a mechanic. Her chubby son, a few years younger than Consuela, poked his head around the door at that point and made a remark to which his mother responded by pretending to box his ears. For this one, she said, she had no hopes at all, her fond looks belying the words. He was idle, good for nothing and cheeky, and again she pretended to cuff his ears while he barely ducked, smiling broadly, secure in her affection for him.

The father arrived soon afterwards and seemed amused to find me enjoying the local wine. He demonstrated the correct way to tackle it from a wineskin, biting off the thin stream in mid-air without a drop being spilt. But in spite of his urging I did not believe it was a skill I could acquire without getting a good deal of the stuff down myself in the process. Arriving at the shrine of St James travel worn and a touch threadbare was perfectly in keeping with the journey, but to turn up copiously stained with red wine would definitely be bad form, I decided, and made the weak excuse of not being able to manage even another drop.

'Thanks be to God for wine that maketh glad the heart

of man,' sang the Psalmist, a sentiment I echoed as I walked down the village street, digesting the *tortilla* before turning in. It warmed the body as well as the heart, and I felt relaxed and happy as I strolled slowly along. It was a lovely clear night, with the stars visible in all their glory. Back at the town hall I discovered that the ground floor was given over to a bar and all eight of the village men were gathered there playing cards. The town's *sello* was produced to stamp my *certificación de paso*, a large involved seal in inverse proportion to the size and importance of the village, and then an older stamp was added for good measure. A drink was courteously offered, but I declined it as clearly this was a male sanctuary, and in any case I thought it wise to make for my bed before the cold of the *refugio* could begin to penetrate. As had become my habit, I read the 'Office of Compline' and said my prayers in my sleeping bag.

I awoke with the first light to a great chorus of twittering birds, and when I poked my head out of the small window I could see flocks of them flitting in and out of the ruined houses. It was a lovely dawn, still and rosy. I set my stove carefully on the floor among the crowded beds, made coffee, and drank it crouched before the low window, not wanting to miss a moment of what was going on outside. The advantage of these early nights with their lack of distractions was that I always awoke at dawn which is a magical hour. Each day began with such a sense of adventure that I could hardly wait to be out on the road. Packing and loading the panniers was the work of a few moments, the drill being so familiar by now. I knew where every item was and could find it in a trice, even in the dark. Then I was out into the bright, cold, fresh-smelling morning.

The soil looked chalky now under the barest sprinkling of green. Belying the poverty of the land, fat rabbits were running about and sunning themselves by the verges. A quail skittered over the threadbare fields, and from every small coppice, hedge and scrap of stone rose the sound of birdsong.

Within a few miles of Hontanas a huge arch hung with stonecrop and clumps of fern spanned the road, looking for all the world like the most expensively contrived ruin in a gentleman's country park. I rode back and forth through it several times before dismounting to examine it more closely. Together with some fragments of wall, it was all that remained of the great Hospital of St Antón, founded in 1146, whose particular speciality was the care of people suffering from 'St Anthony's Fire', or erysipelas, a horrid and painful eruption of the skin, regarded in medieval times as on a par with leprosy and very contagious.

Continuing the idea of a gentleman's park the remains of an avenue of fine specimen trees reached out from the arch on either side of the road. Beyond, towering high above the plain, was a gaunt terraced hill crowned with a ruined fortress, and around its lower slopes clung the small town of Castrojeriz. This had been the site of seven pilgrim hospitals in its medieval heyday, and the history of the place was already old by that time. It had been a notable Roman town and before that the stronghold of local tribes. The land round about showed the strain of this long occupation, appearing ancient and eroded, drained of its fertility.

The town itself was full of character, surprisingly large, and with at least four fine Romanesque churches. As I followed the yellow pilgrim arrows which led me along a lower terrace around the perimeter of the hill, I saw ahead of me a slim figure that for a moment made me think that my eyes were deceiving me. It appeared to be a medieval youth clad in doublet and hose of soft faded tones of ochre and tan, with an elegant version of a pilgrim's wide-brimmed hat. The large modern rucksack, however, quickly dispelled the notion of it being a medieval ghost. When I drew level I discovered an even less likely phenomenon, an American woman who was studying European medieval history and who was walking the *Camino* as a part of her course. Her name was Amy, and she said she never mentioned her studies to anyone back in her home state of Colorado as people there didn't believe there was any history before George Washington. Being in Europe was wonderful, if for no other reason than to be accepted as normal. She had started her walk from the Pyrenees, and like me had stayed in *refugios* along the way, varying this with a night at a *fonda* or small hotel every so often for the luxury of a bath.

Both of us were delighted to meet a fellow pilgrim, and we stopped at a bar for a coffee while we exchanged experiences of the road. Amy removed her boot to ease a painful blister, and as soon as the woman behind the bar noticed this she asked a customer who spoke English to tell us about the 'town healer who cured sick pilgrims'. Intrigued, Amy replaced her boot and, escorted by two young children from the bar, we were taken to a house on an a higher terrace of the town. The children explained about Amy's foot to the young Spaniard who opened the door and he immediately ushered us upstairs to an old-fashioned parlour on the first floor. In a country of cold rooms, this one was particularly chill, but spotlessly clean and sparsely furnished with rather beautiful antique pieces, clearly the room where guests were received. After a while the young man returned with an even younger woman in a dressing gown, carrying between them a bowl of water, soap, towel, a bottle of alcohol and various plasters and bandages. No one spoke while Amy's foot was being bathed and dressed, but afterwards we were taken to the warm pleasant family room and given coffee and biscuits. A plump, jolly older woman, the mother, joined us, together with several other people including the man from the bar, Miguel, to translate for us. Amid shrieks of laughter, lots of embracing and back-slapping, we learnt that the family of three brothers and a sister were all 'healers' having inherited the skill from their father who was now dead. Any pilgrim suffering aches, pains or blisters was tended to the best of their ability, before being sent on their way. Amy's offer of payment, even to donate to a favourite charity, was fiercely refused. It was a privilege, a duty, to look after the pilgrims; there could be no talk of payment. The mother said she often fed pilgrims too. 'Nothing,' she said, echoing the earlier remarks of Father José María, 'was too good for pilgrims.' She couldn't understand the attitude of that terrible village down the road (Hornillos del Camino) who had once refused a pilgrim a glass of water!

One fascinating detail of the house was shown to me by the pretty daughter, still in her dressing gown. Outside on the balcony was the metal door of a long shaft that ran under the floor of the living room. A wood fire was lit in it, and it supplied the underfloor heating to the apartment, a copy of the original Roman hypocaust, confirmed Miguel.

I left Amy at Castrojeriz where I'm sure she had a splendid rest day and pushed on for Frómista. There were several very particular churches in the next few miles which I would be very sad to miss. The pattern about opening hours, as far as there was one, seemed to be that all churches were closed between one and five, while some were never opened, or at least not in April and May.

It was about fifteen miles to Frómista, and I pressed on at more than my usual speed, stopping only at Boadillo del Camino, where a Gothic cross, its shaft covered with scallop shells was far too lovely to not to be admired in detail.

The day was warming up deliciously and I would have been happy to stop more often, but I resisted distractions in the hope of getting to Frómista before locking-up time. I might have known there was no need to hurry, however. Even though it was barely midday when I arrived, the church was firmly locked. Fortunately much of its attraction is the lovely exterior. The Romanesque church of San Martín at Frómista is like no other monument on the *Camino*. It is a beautifully balanced building of a particularly lovely golden stone, with a wealth of terracotta tiled and rounded roofs at differing heights over the apse. Just beneath the eaves is a running frieze made up of several hundred beautifully carved animals, human figures, monsters and plants. It reminded me a little of the marvellous Armenian church of Holy Cross on the island of Akhtamar in Lake Van, except that Frómista's church rises not from an azure lake, but incongruously from an unattractive little square.

While I was studying the frieze from a nearby bench, a coach drove up and about thirty visitors, all middle-aged, got down and milled about the church, showing the same sort of disappointment as I had felt about finding it locked. It is difficult for so large a group of people descending altogether upon a peaceful location not to appear as a minor invasion, and usually I beat a hasty retreat at the approach of coach parties. But this one was noticeably restrained, and as unobtrusive as thirty people can be in an otherwise deserted square. One of their number came over to ask me whether I had located the priest, and went off hopefully to find him. Several others drifted across, and as soon as they discovered I was English, they addressed me in that language with a fluency that made me ashamed of my

ungrammatical French. They were all Belgians, members
of a private travel club whose sole purpose was to organise
cultural holidays, and they were currently exploring the
Camino. Because of the unusual warmth of the day I was
wearing my red Confraternity sweatshirt with its large
black scallop shells and several of the coach party asked
if they might photograph me as I was the first pilgrim they
had seen on the route. This was more embarrassing than
being photographed by tourists in Burgos, for the Belgian
party appeared knowledgeable; they had clearly done their
homework and knew about pilgrims. Did this mean then
that they considered me a certain kind of person? More
religious than the average perhaps? I found myself very
eager to dispel any such notions. 'I was not a pilgrim,
well not in any real sense. I was just going to Santiago,
like them; taking a little longer over the journey that
was all, and doing it by bicycle of course.' But they
were not to be balked of their memento 'Of course it
was different, and they only wished they had the time and
the courage', and so forth. Their organiser returned at this
point, unable to find the key to the church, and we went
our separate ways.

Eight miles beyond Frómista is another tiny village,
Villalcázar de Sirga, which in Picaud's day had been
a thriving town with a great convent under the direct
protection of the Knights Templar. The church of Santa
María is all that remains of the thirteenth-century glory but
that alone is enough to evoke its past. Where Frómista had
a delicate classical perfection, this church was sumptuous in
scale from the vast entrance arch and lovely portal to the
details of tombs and chapels within. I gained access thanks
to the Belgians whose organiser had been successful here in
tracking down the key.

When I had ridden into the village and seen the Belgians' coach parked there, I had tried to escape observation. Having been waved off from Frómista with lots of *Bon voyages* and *Bonne routes* the thought of having to go through it all again made me feel shy. But they had been waiting for me to appear, and to my surprise their organiser came straight over and invited me to have lunch with them. She said they had arranged a very special lunch here in this village and having a pilgrim as their guest would make it truly memorable. I thought they were merely being charitable and friendly, but since both motives were in keeping with the spirit of the pilgrimage, I accepted – no real traveller ever refuses a meal anyway.

The lunch, which turned out to be more in the nature of a banquet, was served in a former sixteenth-century warehouse, a long room with a heavily beamed ceiling and a single table running down the centre. A dear old man, Don Pablo Payo, the owner, was welcoming the guests at the door, dressed in the hat and cloak of a traditional pilgrim, a staff and gourd in one hand and a mayor's heavy chain of office round his neck. Any feeling of it being an over-theatrical production was at once dispelled by his sweetness of expression and his air of it all being the most natural thing in the world. As he handed me a large carnation with which he welcomed all the women, the organiser explained enthusiastically that they had brought along a 'real pilgrim' to their feast. Don Pablo responded that if that was the case then I would be fed and wined for nothing, as that was the custom.

At whose charge finally I dined I am unsure, but there was no doubt as to who was the guest of honour at the feast. The seat at the head of the table was left vacant for St James, and my handlebar bag with its large scallop shell was commandeered to represent him. I didn't write down the details of the meal at the time, and my mind is now a blank about what exactly I ate. I know that it was very good and that course followed course as befits a banquet, and that the wine was served from brown jugs, but all other details escape me because there was so much talk and so many questions to answer. Many of the Belgians were around my age; they put in a lot of time and effort they said to have 'authentic and meaningful holidays', and clearly money was no problem to them. But what I was doing, taking off on my own, travelling under my own steam impressed them as something special. 'How can you take such risks?' they asked. I was at a loss as to how to respond. I have made dangerous journeys, certainly, but I wouldn't have included the Santiago pilgrimage among these, at least not in any physical sense. If there were dangers then they were more subtle, more to do with having ideas challenged, attitudes changed.

After lunch Don Pablo made a great show of stamping my *certificación de paso* as a further object of interest for the tourists, and with everyone just a little glazed with the abundant rich food and wine, we made our final farewells. They would be back in Belgium long before I reached Santiago.

Before I left Villalcázar I had the chance to see the church in more detail when Don Pablo spotted the sacristan and asked him to unlock it again for me. It was a wonderful interior, and I particularly wanted to see again the huge altarpiece painted with scenes from the life of Christ. To do this required the use of a hundred-peseta piece to light it, and when the sacristan saw me fish one out, he snatched it from my hand, pocketed it and substituted a piece of base metal instead. When I left the church, however, he presented me with my second white carnation of the day. I don't know if I would have found all this so delightfully in keeping with the tradition of the pilgrimage had I not been feeling so relaxed and expansive. But in spite of the obvious tourist hype, Villalcázar had provided more sense of the medieval than many other places on the *Camino*, and I rode away from it feeling deeply at peace with my fellow men.

10

Mostly Pilgrims

The splendidly named Carrión de los Condes, a town associated with the legend of El Cid and approved of by Aimery Picaud, was only four miles down the road, but as the celebratory lunch with the Belgians had taken up most of the afternoon, I could not have gone much further. Nor would I have thought it wise to make strenuous efforts on top of such a meal.

The *refugio* was in the house of the parish priest, which adjoined the church of Santa María del Camino whose worn Romanesque carvings on the south portal were supposed to depict the hundred Christian virgins given to the Moors as the yearly tribute before the Battle of Clavijo put an end to the practice. The dormitory was attached to the north wall of the church and had the strange decoration of a row of gargoyles leering above the beds. It was quite a contrast to the flesh pots of Villalcázar, and somehow the austerity of it made me decide it would be a good idea to wash a little more thoroughly than I had been doing recently, even though the water was the same freezing temperature as in most *refugios*. It was an exercise that required a good deal of firmness, especially as I decided to wash my hair as well. The water was so cold that I doubt I could have held my head under the tap long enough to rinse off the shampoo had I not concentrated hard on St Cuthbert and all those ascetic Celtic saints. By the time I finished, it felt as though an iron band had been clamped tightly around my skull.

The reward for this minor mortification of the flesh was that it felt wonderful just to go outside where the temperature was, as usual, several degrees higher than indoors. Picaud describes Carrión de los Condes as 'industrious and prosperous, rich in bread and wine and meat and all fruitfulness.' Its river, the Rio Carrión, was also one to which he gave a clean bill of health. I found it not nearly as memorable or attractive a town as many I'd seen along the way. But it did seem to have remained prosperous and bustling, and the river still flowed below it, with some lovely Benedictine cloisters beyond. There was even a scrap of the medieval town remaining with the Church of Santiago in the middle of it, graced by a superb Christ in Majesty on its west wall. The fact that for once I was in time for mass also made for a closer sense of the continuity of the pilgrimage, although the entire congregation was no more than about twenty persons.

But the next day brought a change. Pushing on across the same desolate plateau that I had reached soon after leaving Burgos, which now seemed weeks, instead of just days ago, I began to understand something of the monotony that other pilgrims had suffered on this stretch. With no blue skies to lighten the harshness of the Castilian landscape, a sense of bleakness overshadowed everything. The sense of joy in the journey had faded. With the prevailing westerly wind once more blowing the dust of the eroding land strongly in my face, it was all once more a struggle, while my mind searched about for distractions.

With my head tucked down out of the wind I did not see the spare figure in shirt sleeves swinging along with staff and knapsack until I was almost level with him. An unmistakable pilgrim, I thought, as I stopped to greet him, and must have said as much, for he turned a fine craggy face towards me and after shaking hands and introducing himself in an unmistakably Dutch accent as Harrie, let me know how he felt about being described as a pilgrim. 'It's the only thing I've not enjoyed about this journey, the cars and buses are stopping all the time to take photographs. Every town I pass through there's someone wanting to photograph a pilgrim. Even the priests say "Come here, because you are a real pilgrim. Come and be photographed with these tourists." But I am not a real pilgrim. I'm walking to Santiago that is all. I hate all this commercialism.'

A conversation that gets off to such a fine impassioned start without any preambles could not, I felt, be abandoned until it had been explored a little further. I suggested we had a drink while we talked. As it was a particularly lonely part of the *Camino* with no bars anywhere near, we sat by the roadside with the thin green wheat fields at our back, shielding the flame of my stove from the wind while the kettle boiled for coffee. Harrie seemed not to feel the cold. He was a sculptor from Leiden, he told me, somewhere in his mid- to late-thirties, I guessed, and appeared very fit, with not a spare ounce of fat on him. He looked, in fact, exactly like someone who had been walking all day and every day for seven weeks, and this included his rather other-worldly expression. In spite of his modern dress I thought he bore an uncanny resemblance to the pilgrims carved on the church door panel at Burgos, and was not

143

surprised that people found him a good subject for their cameras – not an observation I thought it wise to share with Harrie.

He was walking to Santiago, he said, because he had come to a point in his life where he needed 'space to think, to work things out; a time away from everyday problems'. There were not so many places left he thought where you could walk so far through such fine countryside, as well as seeing so many marvellous works of art. The people in the villages and in the bars were charming, and didn't bother you with all this pilgrim business. This was an ideal journey for anyone wanting to walk and think.

Soon after starting off from Le Puy, he said, he had met up with two other men walking the route – a priest from Belgium and a Swiss gynaecologist. They had quickly established a pattern of staying together each night at an agreed rendezvous, usually a *refugio*, but they always walked alone during the day, each valuing, indeed needing their solitude. Harrie said they had met quite a number of other people doing the route, many of them rushing to get to Santiago as fast as possible. He thought it mad to hurry, it was wasting the journey. The travelling was the easy part, you had nothing to worry about; the problems began when you reached the end and took up where you left off. When he started out he said he had far too much in his rucksack, half of it he had sent home: one of the best things about the walk for him so far had been finding how little you really needed.

As we parted company I realised that the day no longer seemed bleak. Meeting Harrie had blown away the cobwebs far more effectively than any cold upland wind. In spite of his determinedly secular approach and his impatience with labels like 'pilgrim', much of what he had said could have come from straight from Bunyan; except that it was expressed in his own unequivocal terms which served to cloak their underlying spirituality. I would have loved to be present at the evening conversations with his companions.

I was still inwardly chuckling at the thought of the tourists' surprise over Harrie's indignant refusals to pose for photographs when I rode into Sahagún, a town whose air of dusty crumbling decay came as a shock. I had been expecting something rather grand and certainly less alien. Once again I had the distinct impression of being back in Asia, only this time it was the streets and buildings that evoked the memory rather than the landscape.

Sahagún had been the site of the most powerful monastery in Spain, at the very centre of Christian expansion and the Reconquest. It had risen to this position in the eleventh century when Alfonso VI decided to subject the earlier foundation to Cluniac reform. Alfonso's confessor, the Benedictine Bernard of Aquitaine, was chosen to bring about the new order, and so well did he succeed that Sahagún soon had over fifty abbeys and priories dependent upon it and was exercising something of the political and religious power and influence that Cluny itself wielded in the Christian world. When Toledo was captured from the Moors in 1086, it was Bernard who became bishop there.

By the time Aimery Picaud was making his pilgrimage in the following century, trade from every corner of Europe had built up a 'prosperous town' around the monastery, one of the high spots of the *Camino Francés*. Sahagún's river also gained Picaud's approval, and his guide reminds pilgrims of the town's connection with Charlemagne and the battle fought there against the Moors when some of his knights' lances were found to have taken root in the ground during the night before the battle and had put forth leaves. This was afterwards said to be a foreshadowing of the palms of martyrdom bestowed upon those warriors who were to be killed in the battle. Poplars growing beside the river are still pointed out as the descendants of those flowering lances.

Trees in a water meadow and a few strange and very beautiful brick churches towering above the mean buildings of a run-down town are all that is left of Sahagún's glory. The foreign feeling of the place was due as much to this extraordinary contrast of decayed grandeur and mean poverty as to the unique architecture of the battered ancient churches. They are in a style known as Mudéjar, having been built by Muslim craftsmen from Islamic Spain. Because there is no stone in these parts, brick was used exclusively in their construction, and the result was more exotic than anything else I had seen so far on the *Camino*. Of the powerful monastery of Sahagún, nothing remains except a few formless lumps, a great arch and a half-ruined chapel, and only four of the nine famous churches seem still to be standing. The small church of San Tirso, standing in an incongruous littered square behind the ruined monastery, has been extensively restored, which enables one to see just how lovely and perfectly balanced the Mudéjar style could be; and how intricate and varied too, in spite of the limitations of working in the single brick medium. Another of the remaining churches, San Lorenzo, with its onion-shaped arches and great square bell tower had not yet been subjected to the restorers, and its general air of dilapidation was somehow more satisfying, as though there was still something of its inner spirit left. But it was the derelict church of La Peregrina on a hill to the west of the city that made the deepest impact. The dedication alone – the portrayal of the Virgin as a pilgrim – was a moving one,

146

with its echoes of the Flight into Egypt, and of the earlier journey, heavy with child, to Bethlehem and the birth of the Son of God in a stable. I had grown used to seeing St James portrayed as a pilgrim journeying to his own tomb. I had even seen Jesus himself depicted as a pilgrim on the Road to Emmaus, but this was the first time I had come across his mother in the role. I found on this journey I was forced constantly to redefine what the word pilgrim meant. It was something that I should have liked to discuss with Harrie.

But the church of La Peregrina would have made a deep impression even without these associations, and I like to think that I would have recognised it for a Franciscan foundation even had I not known it was one. The choice of the site overlooking the city, and the deceptive simplicity of design, coupled with the massive scale of the walls, were typically Franciscan. And beyond the melancholy that hangs over all abandoned buildings there was also a sense of gentle pervading sadness that not even the Mudéjar architecture could hide, and which always seems to mark buildings connected with St Francis. He must have been here himself, for he made a pilgrimage to Santiago in 1214.

I hadn't wanted to eat my midday meal in Sahagún, and as the day had warmed up a little I bought food for a picnic instead. As soon as I was clear of the town, I stopped for the second time that day by the side of the road to boil up my kettle and to set out my meal of bread, anchovies, olives, tomatoes and fruit. A meal is a natural time for counting blessings, which is perhaps how the custom of saying a grace before meals began. But rather than thankfulness for the food, I found myself thinking about the people I had met on this pilgrimage, especially

147

since crossing the Pyrenees. On no other journey could I remember so many warm encounters. Even quite casual exchanges had so often seemed to carry an extra quality, a gratuitous kindness – like buying a stamp an hour before in Sahagún's post office where the clerk shyly tried out his few words of English, purely, I felt at the time, to make me feel at home. Since these roadside halts were also opportunities for writing up my notes, I find mixed in among the descriptions of Sahagún, musings about fellow pilgrims and people encountered along the way, and at the end of the jumble is the question, 'Is this why the *Camino* is like no other road?'

It was to be the last interval for quiet reflection that I would enjoy for the next few hours. After lunch conditions deteriorated immediately. The brief golden spell which had burnished the brick of Sahagún's ancient churches had disappeared behind low grey cloud. The *Camino* proper had taken off on its lonely cross-country route where once wolves devoured pilgrims rash enough to be travelling alone. Even without the wolves, it had remained an empty quarter, traversed only by a parlous track that was not negotiable with a laden touring bicycle. I am pleased to say that this sad state of affairs has since been rectified with the extensive rebuilding and resurfacing of this section of the *Camino*. Cyclists need no longer dice with death as I did that afternoon on one of the most horrible trunk roads it has ever been my misfortune to hazard my life.

The N120 was bad enough, but when I turned right onto the N601 I could only think that I was being required to serve my term in purgatory immediately. Aggravated by a vicious side wind, the wash from the great roaring trucks was almost more than I could cope with, and Roberts shied and skittered about like an unbroken colt. Finally, the inevitable happened; in the wash of a particularly huge speeding monster Roberts and I became temporarily airborne, left the road altogether and landed in scrubland quite a way to our right, my head missing a large boulder by a hair's breadth. A farm worker, the only other cyclist I had seen all day, had been riding close behind me making the most of the small bit of shelter I offered and he stopped to disentangle me from Roberts. To the surprise of us both, I think, I proved to be unscathed except for a bruised thigh. I continued on to Mansilla trying to sing 'He Who Would Valiant Be' to give me courage.

Mansilla de las Mulas has the substantial remains of its medieval adobe walls still in place and, apart from the intrusion of the N601 which thunders through the middle of it, is a peaceful little town beside the River Esla, with storks nesting in a couple of towers left from some ancient building, the bulk of which has vanished. This was where I intended to spend the night if I could locate the *refugio*, not always an easy task. After asking several people, the owner of the flower shop sent me off with her young son on his bike to escort me to the priest's house. As is the way with small boys, he called out to his friends along the way, so that by the time we reached the priest's open door I had a sizeable escort. The priest seemed rather a surly character, fond neither of pilgrims nor small boys. The boys scattered and I was left alone to be interrogated. I knew enough Spanish by now to point out that I was a *peregrina*, not a *peregrino*, and this brought a rough tirade down on my head, the gist of which was 'Why are you disguised as a man then?' Clearly he had never heard of 'rational cycling dress'. Still my *credenciales* were impeccable, so he could do nothing but stamp them, his lips a thin line of disapproval. My escort then reassembled to race me to the *refugio*. This turned out to be a substantial range of old buildings in a back street grouped around a roughly tiled courtyard entirely filled with a large fig tree. It was a charming place, but in the middle of a major refurbishment. All the walls had just been repainted with a great deal of enthusiasm which had sent the paint flying over the beds and floor and anything else in the way. A general sweep out would have improved it no end, but they were clearly not expecting pilgrims just yet.

The little man who showed me around seemed very bossy and emphasised every point he wished to make about the light, water and keys by poking his forefinger at my chest, a habit which always irritates me. But now, tired, bruised, traffic-savaged and sneered at by the chauvinist priest, I found it insufferable and finally told him so unequivocally. Immediately I was sorry, remembering what I had been writing about the sense of communion that is felt on the road; how easy it had seemed to see the reflection of God in everyone when things were going well, and how quickly all that can evaporate under pressure.

Left alone I followed instructions and managed to coax a little warm water into a sort of hip bath in a dark windowless little shed. Grime and lack of amenities notwithstanding, that lukewarm bath was luxury in the context of the *Camino*. I felt renewed, ready for anything. I was sitting on the cleanest spot I could find on a top bunk, wearing all my clothes and sipping a restorative whisky from my diminishing store, when the little man came back.

'*Ubi caritas et amore, Deus ibi est,*' I had just been reading in my prayer book – where there is love and charity, there is God.

The people of the town, he said, had decided it was too cold for me to stay here. They had built another wing of the *Casa Peregrino*, to be officially opened in a month. I would

Fromista

Cloisters at San Marce Leon

Memorial at El Acebo to a cycling pilgrim who suffered a fatal accident on the road to Santiago

Templar castle, Ponferrada

Church of Tricastela Galicia

Twelfth-century tympanum, Santiago

Obradoiro facade of the Cathedral, Santiago

Hospital de los Reyes Católicos – now a luxury parador hotel

be the first to sleep in it, very *tranquilo*, the only one there. He helped me gather my things which had been scattered around by this time, and unlocked a door in the courtyard, throwing it open with a theatrical flourish. My goodness, what a contrast! Instant luxury. Twenty-four bunks, cheek by jowl, each with its pretty flounced quilt and each with a glass and gilt shelf for possessions pilgrims might need in the night.

There was a television room, a kitchen with all 'mod cons' including washing machine, and three luxuriously appointed bathrooms. Dimmer switches, net curtains, easy chairs and deep springy carpets added up to four- or even five-star luxury in my book. I found it daunting and would have much preferred the simplicity of my original quarters. Also, ironically, this splendid new wing was right on the main road with its thundering trucks. But I had no choice in the matter. This was what the town thought modern pilgrims deserved. More importantly, it was an expression of their *caritas*, and the little man (trying hard not to poke his finger at me) demonstrated each new wonder as though he personally was making me a gift of it.

11

A City Full of Delights

The walls of Mansilla de las Mulas seen from across the river
made a suitably medieval start to the day, an impression of
period which continued as I set off into the wide empty
countryside on a narrow road alongside the northern bank
of the Esla. I had almost decided against making this long
detour to visit the church of San Miguel de Escalada. It
would add twenty miles to the journey, and unless it
dropped, most of them into the teeth of the west wind
which continued to be as wicked as ever. I felt stiff from
yesterday's tumble and I wanted to get to León where I
could have a rest day. It was only when I recalled what
the 'reluctant pilgrim', Harrie, had said the day before
about wasting the journey by hurrying, that I decided I
must take the opportunity to see this unique monument.
Anyway, the wind could well die down before I had to turn
around and face it; or, hope being the bedrock of travellers,
it could even change direction at the same time as I did and
continue to blow in my favour.

Whatever the outcome, it was a wonderfully exhilarating
run out eastward to San Miguel. I even had to apply
the brakes in the isolated little adobe villages I passed

for fear of causing casualties among the straying hen population.

San Miguel de Escalada is the largest Mozarabic church in Spain and it stands at the end of the little road, quite alone among green fields, its grey stone walls and tall tower appearing at first sight not unlike the ancient Celtic oratories of Ireland. The closer I came to it, however, the more impressive it appeared and quite unlike anything else I had seen. There must once have been a considerable monastery there, but now only the church itself remains, skilfully restored and very beautiful. I hadn't known what to expect, but I would certainly have been sorry to miss it.

It was built early in the tenth century by Christian craftsmen who had been living in Islamic Spain, and although the Moorish influence is clear in details such as the horseshoe arches, the Mozarabic style, as it is known, is quite different to the Mudéjar architecture that I had seen at Sahagún. San Miguel was a stone structure of great lightness and delicacy, particularly its cloisters and the forest of lovely slender columns inside, which is also typical of Islamic architecture. In many ways the interior reminded me strongly of the Galilee chapel in Durham Cathedral which also has a strong Eastern influence and appears equally strange and fascinating. The Roman Rite was only finally adopted throughout Spain in the eleventh century; before that time Constantinople was still the centre of Christendom and local versions of the Eastern Rite held sway. This was reflected here in the columns forming a division between the chancel and the body of the church which would have carried the iconostasis – a focus for devotion and a barrier to preserve the mysteries of the sanctum from the eyes of the uninitiated – a detail which made the building seem even more exotic.

Lovely as the place was it also reflected, as Sahagún had done, the sad division between two great faiths, since the genius of both was so plainly visible in this building. Christianity and Islam have been in a state of outright war or armed neutrality for so long that the common ground that should exist between them remains largely unexplored. Yet Western and Islamic scholarship and art have so influenced one another over the centuries that they are, as in these churches, inseparably linked. It seems to me that it is in the common misconceptions of great faiths and ideas that destructive forces are able to work. How far, I wondered, did such twisted concepts as St James 'Godly' Moor Slayer, or the teaching of 'Better dead than not a Muslim' underlie such appalling actions as the 'ethnic cleansing' going on today in the Balkans and in Israel?

The wind force and direction remaining equally implac-able, I paid for the effortless ride out to San Miguel, by a muscle-cracking, twenty-mile struggle to León, and when I reached the outskirts, with its acres of soulless looking high-rise flats, it seemed hardly worth the effort. Where was the marvellous city I had been led to expect? Shelter, rest and food seemed more urgent requirements than sight-seeing at this stage, however, and it was the *refugio* that I was most eager to locate, so I pushed on towards the centre of the city in search of it. I stopped once when I caught sight of the small church of St Anna, marooned and overshadowed among the towering buildings. The priest was just locking up after mass, but he kindly stamped my card and pointed out the one slab of medieval fresco that remained after the recent modernisation. After that, I was soon through the worst of the daunting periphery and then many tempting sights did indeed present themselves, including the splendid walls of León, but for once I was tired enough to be able to resist them.

Whether the *refugio* actually existed I never really found out, because in the process of trying to discover its whereabouts among the extensive restoration work in the monastery of San Isidoro, I was kidnapped by a lovely man called Paco who took me off to stay with his wife and two small children in a modest apartment at the foot of the old solid walls of León. Paco had the habit of carrying off people. When he was a penniless young man seeing the world, he had done a short stint as a waiter in a Swiss hotel. At one of the tables he had met his future wife, Christina, a young Swiss girl on holiday with her parents. Whirlwind romance though it was, it seemed to have worked. Apart from the language, and an occasional moan about Spanish housing and education, Christina said she had never regretted her choice. Giving her the opportunity to speak French again with another woman was one of the reasons Paco had advanced for inviting me to stay. The other was that he was using the *refugio* for his tools. Paco was in charge of a work opportunity scheme for young people which tackled some of the necessary restoration on the fabric of the old city, and currently he was in the middle of a large-scale project on the monastery of San Isidoro. I could not have found a more knowledgeable guide to León's historic buildings, nor a more warmly welcoming family. My much-needed rest day extended to a three nights' stay, and even then I had trouble getting away, as Christina and Paco tried to tempt me with offers of trips to the seaside and with fresh aspects of their city that I had not yet seen.

I would have been happy in León wherever I had stayed, and Aimery Picaud's assessment of it was one I wholeheartedly endorsed. Although no longer 'the residence of the king and the court', it was certainly still 'full of all delights'. The variety that was packed within the compass of its splendid walls never ceased to amaze me. The narrow little alleyways meandering up and down, through arches and around corners until I lost all sense of direction would debouch suddenly into open spaces. There appeared to be no end to these squares which were of every shape and size. Some contained nothing but their own sense of spaciousness, always surprising after the tunnel-like approach. Others were lined with an assortment of pleasant old buildings. Tall period houses, some extremely fine, and many hung with wooden balconies leaning companionably against one another, their roofs all at different levels. Shops, restaurants and bars – particularly bars – were squeezed in between them in great profusion. Indeed bars were such a speciality of León that I could well believe the claim that you could visit a different one daily for a year and still not have seen them all. Weekly markets also added their bustle to many of León's larger squares during the hours of daylight. Altogether, I thought it impossible not to be captivated by the place.

My serious visits fitted naturally into this pleasant wandering. Fine churches and buildings of architectural interest, like the Gaudí house, are scattered throughout the old walled city, clustered like the lesser jewels in a crown around the great diadems of the cathedral and the basilica of San Isidoro. León's third great gem, San Marcos, the former headquarters of the Knights of Santiago is some way outside the old walls and has been turned into a luxury hotel. The most outstanding feature of this opulent monument, built at the height of the Order's power and wealth is the Renaissance façade, the longest in Spain – a hundred metres of elegantly pilastered and pedimented white stone, thickly encrusted with carvings, decorations and portrait heads. It is in the Spanish plateresque style which, like the work of silversmiths from which the name is derived, is very fine and intricate, and the general effect is more like a giant tapestry than a work in stone. I spent a pleasant afternoon in San Marcos visiting the museum and the elegant cloisters, but much as I enjoyed it for its own sake, I lost the sense of the *Camino* there; it was altogether too grand and the period too late. The main attraction of San Marcos for a pilgrim is that it is built beside the old medieval bridge across the River Bernesga where the original and more humble pilgrim's hostel of San Marcos once stood.

The great Romanesque basilica of San Isidoro on its prominent mound is the true heart of the city. The name León is a corruption of legion, for the Roman Seventh Legion was stationed here, and the ruins of their temple lie beneath the basilica, as does a succession of Christian churches, one of which was razed by the Moor, Al-Mansur. San Isidoro was built between 1054 and 1066 when the city was being established as the seat of the kings of León, and it replaced a church that was considered not grand enough for its new role. In the days of the relic cult, no new church could be founded without an authenticated bone or two, and for this august building the remains of San Isidoro were procured. A former archbishop of Seville who had died a few centuries earlier, San Isidoro might not immediately suggest the necessary charisma for such a position. He was not an apostle, nor had he been martyred; in fact he seems to have led an uneventful and blameless life. But he did have the advantage of having been a scholar in an age where illiteracy was the norm and had left behind him a reputation for sanctity, as well as a considerable number of learned tracts and treatises which were still being consulted centuries later. More importantly perhaps, he was readily available and needed only to be disinterred from his tomb in Seville's cathedral. No doubt the Moors who had control of Seville at this time valued the princely sum of money which changed hands over the deal more than they needed Isidoro.

I liked the vast solid structure far more from the outside than from within, but the church was also designed to contain the royal pantheon of the kings of León and without doubt it is this lovely vault that is the real joy of the place. There was nothing funereal about it at all, even the tombs were hardly noticeable. The glorious Romanesque frescoes which cover the low-groined vaulting take all one's attention, transporting one immediately into the world of Chaucer and Piers Plowman. The central Christ in Majesty is strikingly Byzantine and arresting in its power. In contrast all around it are simple natural country scenes of shepherds and dogs, trees blowing in the wind, oxen ploughing, goats fighting. Every detail is carefully tied in to the total pattern and effect and yet there is a tremendous sense of freedom about the work too. It is skilfully painted with all the vigour of medieval humour and inventiveness. Apart from the beauty of the work, what made it seem so extraordinary was the way in which the angelic world had been worked into these scenes of everyday life – like the Annunciation to the shepherds – with no division, no different technique or colour, or the odd lily, as became the custom in later ages. The natural and the supernatural worlds existed side by side in an apparently easy unself-consciousness. Had the artist been less able, it might have been seen as naivety of execution, but with such consummate artistry this could not have been the case. It made me realise how much closer medieval man

159

was in spirit, as well as in time, to the Gospel events. How easily he could accept it all. Looking at his world displayed in this pantheon, I envied him his innocence.

For a city the size of León to be blessed with San Isidoro would seem to be sufficient, but in addition it boasts a cathedral which many people consider to be the finest in Spain. By great good fortune my visit to León had coincided with a performance of Mozart's Requiem Mass in the cathedral. I miss music very much when I am travelling, and the opportunity to hear such a work on this journey, especially in such a setting, was not to be missed. One of the problems of the pilgrimage to Compostela is the sheer wealth of ecclesiastical masterpieces along the way; the eye can only take in so much, and it is all too easy to become satiated with the sheer richness of it all. By this time even a fine uncluttered Gothic cathedral needed something more than an airy lightness and a soaring harmony of line to make a real impression. León's cathedral, consecrated in 1303 is French Gothic rather than Spanish, and is reminiscent of Chartres in that lovely as the architecture is, the true glory of the place is its vast expanses of stained glass. But where Chartres' glass is predominately blue and red, that of León is also purple, green and yellow, and all shades in between. It is arguably the most wonderful glass anywhere, and in this respect was certainly like no other church I have ever seen. To sit there as day turned slowly into evening with these marvellous windows ablaze as though with celestial fire, and with Mozart's Gloria ringing out from the choir gave another dimension to the idea of worship.

It was raining lightly when I left León, and scores of storks were circling around the cathedral, coming down from their airy perches in a graceful spiralling descent. Together with their huge untidy nests balanced so absurdly on the points of pinnacles and turrets, they are my lasting memory of this splendid cathedral.

As I rode out of the city across the narrow medieval bridge besides San Marcos, I was feeling rather the worse for wear. The two and a half days in León had been far more exhausting than any battling with headwinds, possibly because Christina, Paco and I had stayed up every night chatting in a mixture of languages until two a.m. I came back to the comparative peace and quiet of the *Camino* as to an old taciturn friend with whom one could happily keep silent.

Back on the old faithful N120, there was little distraction in the twenty-five miles to Astorga. I stopped only twice in fact, once was at the old sanctuary of the Virgen del Camino, patroness of León, where the new building replacing the original sixteenth-century structure seemed absolutely in keeping with the ugly characterless architecture of León's spreading suburbs. The modern sculptures on the façade were much too good for such a setting, I thought. They are a line of large rough bronzes of the apostles, including St James, and are, I think, a representation of Pentecost and the descent of Holy Fire. The emaciated figures all facing squarely towards Santiago seemed to be waving a goodbye and godspeed to the departing pilgrims.

The second stop was at Puente de Orbigo, a small town with an extraordinary Romanesque bridge, so long that every book I read on the subject gives it a different length, varying from 104 to 205 metres! All accounts agree, however, on it being supported by twenty arches, so I think the longer tally must be right. Most of these arches stand on dry ground, and the Orbigo has either shrunk dramatically since the Romans first built the bridge or, more probably, it was made that length in order to clear marshland that flanked the river.

Walking the bridge gives a tremendous feeling of the medieval *Camino* if only because it is a paved way denied to traffic. Far more than on an ancient track, you cannot but be aware of your feet treading the same grooves as did all the other pilgrims. I read that famous jousts had been held in the centre of the bridge in the late Middle Ages, and that would certainly have been a novel spectacle since there was not room for two horses to pass, and the defeated knight would have likely ended up in the river.

Astorga was the next significant place on the route, but somehow, in spite of its rather exciting ramparts, I did not take to it at all. Perhaps coming so close on the heels of León it did not have much chance. There was certainly some interesting architecture, apart from the massive Roman walls, not least the Bishop's Palace built by Gaudí in 1910. It houses the museum of the *Camino* now, but this, characteristically, was closed, so I could only admire the elaborate Gothic fantasy of Gaudí's exterior which complemented the extravagance of the adjoining cathedral roof line, a splendid pot-pourri of fantastic statuary and ornamentation. The cathedral itself was open, but it had been de-commissioned and was now a lifeless dusty museum, poorly endowed and haphazardly arranged. The ticket kiosk was selling hideous souvenirs, including Scottish dolls in tartan. Still none of this really explains my dislike of Astorga.

Sometimes it is possible to arrive at a place on quite the wrong day. Another day might have been quite different and yielded many pleasures, but on the wrong day nothing will go well. So it was with my visit to Astorga: I could not even find lunch there. After circling the town several times, I finally gave up and began to search equally hard for the route onwards. When finally I came upon the familiar, worn yellow arrow, I departed thankfully.

Almost instantly the day improved. I was on a narrow country road heading upwards into the hills under a brightening sky. Ahead of me was the crossing of the mountains of León, through the heart of the region known as the Maragateria. A few miles out a turning to the right brought me into the cobble-stoned village of Castrillo de los Polvazares, a show case of a village, self-consciously restored to its original state – except that no mountain village would ever look so uniformly immaculate, or have its animal feeding troughs planted with flowers. But chic though it was, and used mostly as holiday homes for city folk, it had a splendid restaurant where my spirits were restored with a bowl of thick soup and a plate of delicious locally cured ham.

After that, the day improved still further. As the road continued to climb, gently enough not to be too taxing, the landscape grew progressively wilder. To crown my enjoyment the sun finally broke through the cloud and added a rich flush of colour to the scene. The few villages I passed through did not have the polished look of Castrillo de los Polvazares and were all the more attractive for that. But many of the squat stone houses were empty, and it was clear that life here was at the end of an era; an ageing population had seen the younger generation depart to different lives and occupations. There seemed little farming other than animal husbandry in this broken hill country, and it was difficult to imagine how a large population had ever supported itself.

By late afternoon, after endless stops to admire the constantly changing windswept panoramas I arrived at the village of Rabanal del Camino where I knew that the Confraternity of St James was converting the old priest's house into a *refugio*. It was not finished yet so I would not be able to stay the night there, but while I was admiring the newly restored façade, a woman from the house next door came out and, finding that I was English, invited me in for tea.

Charo and Asumpta were known in the village as *las madrileñas*, the ladies from Madrid. They had discovered Rabanal a few years back, and had been so charmed by it and its position that they had decided to come and live there. Both were scholars and they had brought their extensive library with them and they worked there on various projects. They were equally interested in the countryside and in conservation work, and planted trees, grew vegetables and altogether did more than I could take in during one conversation. Of all the people I had met on the *Camino*, Charo and Asumpta were two I would have liked to have spent more time with. It was they who explained the immediate history of these high Maragatos villages to me.

As I had suspected, this rough hill country had never been able to support communities without some additional income. In the days of the Roman occupation, only the lower sheltered valleys were worked and mining for gold and other metals was the chief interest. The Maragatos who settled the area some time after the collapse of the Roman Empire were thought to descendants of Visigoths. The men had become the traditional muleteers, transporting merchandise all over Spain, while the women had worked the small holdings and looked after the sheep and cows. With the advent of the railways, the long-distance mule trains largely disappeared overnight, and the exodus of the mountain people began. In wilder places, that the railways could not reach, there remained some need for animal haulage, but motorised traffic soon ended that, and still more of the population was forced to leave. There were fewer than thirty souls altogether now in Rabanal.

But in the summer, when the pilgrims poured through, the tiny population was host to as many as two hundred visitors a night, and the water supply dried up. 'Only the summers are horrible here,' said Charo forthrightly. And fearing I might think she disliked pilgrims in general, added quickly that pilgrims who came in the spring or autumn, or even the winter, the 'real pilgrims', were always welcome. 'We enjoy having interesting people to talk to,' said Asumpta, 'but such numbers as come in summer are an invasion.'

Even so they had nothing but praise for the Confraternity of St James who were their next door neighbours. They had come to know some of them well from the working parties which had laboured away there, rebuilding the ruined priest's house and converting it into one of the finest *refugios* of the route. They unlocked it so that I could see over it, and when I realised the extent of what had been accomplished I felt a new sense of pride in being a member of such an enterprising organisation. A lot of thought had gone into the planning, as well as an extraordinary amount of hard work, not to mention the fund raising to pay for it all. The accommodation was appropriately simple, but it was attractive too and had all the necessities, like a place to wash clothes and, equally important I thought, there was a room set aside for reading and quiet reflection, furnished with a small library. And although there was no obvious religious imagery anywhere, there appeared to be a real spiritual dimension to the place. This might have been there before the Confraternity came of course, but it had certainly not been destroyed by anything they had done to the building. I thought it was exactly the sort of *refugio* pilgrims needed. The only problem with it, I gathered, was that it had been decided that it must have a resident warden, and this would mean it could not be open at the bleaker end of the year when the 'real pilgrims' could use it.

'The reason that Rabanal is special,' said Asumpta, breaking into my thoughts, 'is because of the pilgrimage. For eleven hundred years and more there has been this great passage of pilgrims through this place and it has left its mark. Rabanal del Camino was on one of the hardest and most dangerous parts of the route, and a special atmosphere has been created here, you can feel it.' And indeed, I was sure that I could. But if it was the passage of all these pilgrims which had made it so special, then why were large numbers of modern pilgrims so intrusive? 'Because they are not pilgrims,' said Charo forthrightly. 'In summer the atmosphere is quite different. They are in big groups, very noisy; many come in cars. For many it is just a cheap holiday. The real pilgrims get swallowed up in these crowds.' Which sounded very like an echo of what Madame Debril had been saying in St Jean-Pied-de-Port.

Even without the very special atmosphere, Rabanal was a most attractive village, not unlike the over-prettified Castrillo de los Polvazares, but real and lived in. The single unmade street was lined with thick-walled stone houses, whose roofs were wide-eaved to protect the wooden balconies and secluded patios – typical mountain houses, in fact, but with their own regional character. At their back a surprising amount of sheltered land was planted with fruit trees and vegetable plots. Halfway along its length the street opens out into a small dirt square with a tiny church of the Romanesque period built in the same rough, dry-stone construction as the houses. This small square is where the Confraternity's refuge stands and was clearly the original heart of the village. But in recent times a more modern road had been put through on a parallel course fifty yards to the left.

Chonina's bar stands at the side of this narrow tarmac road with ample parking space in front of it, and this newer centre of village life was my next port of call. It was the only place where pilgrims could sleep when I was there, if they were too feeble to cope in the dilapidated old *refugio*. I often make the excuse that my blood has been thinned by my various desert crossings, and certainly I feel the cold more than I used to. I had thought it chilly enough in León, but up at this altitude, once the thin wintry sunshine had been swallowed up in the mountain mists, it was freezing. Having been shown the *refugio* in the old school, I knew I could have survived a night there if I had to, but was most relieved that Chonina could find a corner for me in her small house. And wonder of wonders who should I see as I walked into the tiny bar but Harrie, the 'reluctant pilgrim' and his two companions whose long legs had been eating up the miles while I had been wallowing in the flesh pots of León.

I was introduced to his companions, Guillaume, the gynaecologist from Switzerland, a slim man with exquisite manners and the gentlest of smiles who encouraged everyone else to talk while saying surprisingly little himself, and Paul, a rather stout and argumentative Belgian priest, who was at least twenty years older than the other two and who was treated by them with a mixture of pride and affection and a little gentle mockery. Harrie and Guillaume had rooms at Chonina's, but Paul was sleeping in the *refugio*. 'He takes the pilgrimage very seriously,' Harrie said. 'He thinks he has to suffer which is why he carries twice as much as he needs.' I saw what he meant the following morning as the other two helped to heave the huge rucksack onto Paul's back. He seemed an old-fashioned Christian, for whom suffering would certainly have its reward in heaven, but I didn't think that was why he was carrying such a load. Although he had been ordained a priest, he had worked all his life as a teacher until he retired a few months before. The Santiago pilgrimage was something he had been planning for a long time, and burden and blisters notwithstanding, he seemed to me to be enjoying it as much as anyone. He had had very little opportunity for holidays he said, and had really gone to town on all sorts of gadgetry with which camping shops tempt the young and unwary – like a massive knife with twenty-one blades, self-igniting matches, heavy torches and so on – no wonder his rucksack weighed a ton.

No sooner had we sat down and Chonina had brought in the soup than Paul began to ask me what a Protestant like me was doing on pilgrimage. 'Or are you a heathen like these other two?' he joked. At the other few tables in the tiny bar locals sat drinking, cracking jokes, playing dominoes. The inevitable television rumbled on in a corner ignored by all. Chonina bustled about between kitchen and bar, and every few minutes the door opened and someone else squeezed in or out. 'Even in this noise and when we are trying to eat our food,' said Guillaume tenderly, 'Paul seriously expects us to discuss questions of theology.' All of us saw the joke at the same time, just as Chonina chose the moment to set down a plate of pigs' trotters in front of us, which at the time also seemed uproariously funny. The effort of subduing our laughter and restoring the atmosphere to one suitable for appreciating this speciality of the house ended talk of any sort for a while.

When supper was over there was an attempt to return to the topic of 'real pilgrims', but little came of it. Words like 'religious' and 'spiritual' meant different things to each of us, and perhaps Harrie was wise to refuse to use such labels. When he had first told me about his travelling companions I thought they sounded an unlikely trio. Meeting them together had only reinforced that impression. The three came from such different backgrounds, and their interests and attitudes were also so diverse as to make it highly unlikely they would ever have met outside the thread of the *Camino*. Yet along the way they had developed the sort of understanding and sympathy towards one another that comes usually only after a long acquaintance. Each seemed able to pursue his own line of thought without interfering with the other two, as though the differences that ordinarily make up our lives had become of no importance.

As Harrie said, 'You see life differently when you are walking to Santiago. There's no time, no distance. You have the chance to find out what really matters.' Which, when I thought about it in my cold little bedroom afterwards, seemed no bad description of pilgrimage.

12

Wild Dogs and Wilder Descents

Rugged though conditions were at Chonina's *fonda* – even a little hot water for a bucket bath could be obtained only by negotiation – it was nonetheless a haven in the wilderness. Ahead lay the ascent of the Pass of Foncebadón and the long trek through the unpeopled hills. Any form of civilisation would be rare now until I descended into the valley of Ponferrada. The modest breakfast of a few dry crackers and a cup of coffee was not the best start to what would be a strenuous day.

Much as I looked forward to the passage through the hills, I parted from my companions with some regret, for it was unlikely that we would meet up again on this journey. As I started on the ascent I could hear Paul, who had set off first, singing a '*Venite Sancti Spiritus*' as he swung along on the parallel track. I wished I had as true and tuneful a voice, not that I could have joined in; I needed all my breath to get going on the fifteen hundred foot ascent. Starting on a steep climb first thing in the morning always seems a most terrible effort. For the first ten minutes or so I am convinced it is impossible and that I will have to give up and walk. My lungs feel as though they are on fire and my legs have no strength in them at all. But if I can keep going past the ten-minute point I usually find I have settled into a rhythm, and after that it is much easier. Then if I am alone I do sing, no matter how untunefully, just for the sheer joy of being alive and in the mountains.

I stopped just before the summit to make a detour through the village of Foncebadón, which lies a little to the left of the road. This village appears to be totally abandoned at first sight, but I knew from *las madrileñas* that a mother and her unmarried son were still living there. The mother often joked with Asumpta that she or Charo should marry her son and produce a family to repopulate the village.

I had also been warned about the fierce dogs of Foncebadón and had my 'Dog Dazer' at the ready. Dogs are a problem in many countries, especially now that so many people keep guard dogs that they cannot control. Cyclists particularly suffer from them; even dogs which are usually quite placid can be vicious towards cyclists – no one quite knows why. Over the years I have tried all sorts of ploys to deal with the canine menace. The latest was this 'Dazer', a device that gives out a high-frequency sound which is beyond the range of the human ear, but which dogs can receive, and which they are supposed to find very off-putting. I had yet to try it out on one.

Foncebadón was a strange and eerie place. It had more the feeling of a film set than a village, for the land all about look quite wild and uncultivated. The single street stretched on bleakly for quite some distance, lined with houses on either side, many of which still appeared habitable, though all wore the effects of decay and long neglect, and some had daylight showing through the roofs. The surface of the unmade road was in a parlous state, with deep trampled mud in many places and large rocks breaking through the surface elsewhere; so that is was not easy to wheel Roberts through. As I began to pass between the houses I saw that many of them were used as shelters for animals. From windows and doorways that had been roughly patched and secured, faces of sheep and cows gazed out at me as though wondering who was this stranger. There was not a human to be seen; it felt strange and uncanny.

Then ahead I saw the dogs, quite a posse of them, though I didn't waste time trying to count them. They looked big and threatening, and at least two of them wore wide collars with three-inch spikes sticking out of them like a menacing ruff. They started to pace stiff-legged and alert as I approached. I felt less than confident, but as I could see no escape route, I had no choice but to go on. The one that came for me first was not the most frightening. It was a poor thin Alsatian bitch, her ribs prominent and the erect hair around her neck and shoulders sparse and caked with mud. As she lowered her head and muzzle towards me and snarled her challenge, I pointed the Dazer and pressed the button. As much to my surprise as to hers, I think, she backed off immediately, shaking her head as though to rid it of something unpleasant. The others circled round, still stiff-legged but keeping their distance. I pressed the Dazer in their direction a few more times, and that was the end of the confrontation. They slunk off slowly, and I was left feeling absurdly sorry for them because they were all so thin and in such poor condition. All the same, the incident gave me a confidence about dealing with dogs that I had never possessed before.

As I passed what was left of the primitive little church of Foncebadón I could see that its bell was still hanging in the ruined belfry. A middle-aged man was letting the cows out, their warm breath heavy in the cold air. He nodded an unsmiling response to my greeting, and I continued on to join the road once more, wondering if there could ever be a reprieve for this ghost village before it disappeared completely beneath the grass and bracken.

As I curved back to the road from Foncebadón, the mist came down and the air was suddenly full of moisture. Visibility shrank abruptly to a few feet and the wide view over the way I had just ascended vanished together with the village. The famous iron cross on its tall pole which marks the start of the pass loomed up before me out of the greyness. Traditionally every pilgrim passing the spot adds their stone to the mound on which the cross stands. Ahead of me lay what had always been one of the most fearful passages of the pilgrimage, so much so that Aimery Picaud included a short chapter in his guide to record the names of the men who had repaired the road from Rabanal in the twelfth century and who rebuilt the bridge over the River Miño which a Queen Urraca had destroyed. In some respects the dangers were as real today for a walker or a bicyclist. I added my stone and took the opportunity to don my rain gear. I also read aloud the medieval prayers for the safety of pilgrims.

'O God, Who didst bring Abraham, Thy servant, out of Ur of the Chaldeans, and did preserve him unhurt through all the paths of his pilgrimage . . . Be unto us a covering in the rain and cold, a staff in slippery places . . .'

In spite of the mist, which was as wet as rain, I thought I had better not wear the hood of my rain jacket so that I would have more chance of hearing the approach of any vehicle. The road was very narrow and twisting, with blind corners and steep descents, hazardous at any time, but with such minimal visibility it was extremely dangerous. And indeed I did meet a car on one corner, but fortunately the driver was feeling his way with due caution and I had time to pull off the road; there certainly was not room for us both.

After a few miles of straining to hear above the sound of the tyres and the rustle of the waterproofs – sounds a rider is usually unaware of, but magnified now by the mist – I came over the true summit of the pass and began to lose height. Abruptly I was out of the cloud, as though passing through a curtain to find a new smiling countryside spread out below and the small village of El Acebo at my feet. I had ridden through the middle of two tiny ghost villages in the mist, but El Acebo was still very much alive and in good repair, its roofs newly slated and its small balconies and outside staircases far more solid than they appear in old photographs. The road had also been renewed and I had cause to be thankful that I came to it in clear visibility for it constituted the most potentially lethal hundred yards of the entire descent. The steep slope had been given a concrete finish, roughened to prevent animals slipping, but with a chevron of deeply cut drains running right across it from the houses to a wide gully down the centre of the road. A narrow wheel could find a hundred places to jam or spin off course: it could almost have been designed as the perfect bicycle trap, and for good measure the entire surface was slippery with fresh cow pats. Not much will induce me to walk downhill, but El Acebo did, and even so I had the greatest difficulty getting through without my feet skidding from under me. Just beyond the village was a metalwork sculpture of an upended bicycle, the memorial to one 'Heinrich Krause, Peregrino', a cycling pilgrim who met his death here.

By this time, with all the hard work of the ascent and no proper breakfast I was famished. So, in the manner of the Etruscans and Ancient Egyptians who honoured their dead by having picnics at their tombs, I paid my respects to the memory of a fellow cyclist by brewing up a cup of coffee there and eating what few bits and pieces of stale bread, nuts and dried apricots I had left in my panniers. It was a salutary reminder, if one was needed, of what I had thought at the Foncebadón cross – that modern pilgrims met their share of danger too. Had my guardian angel been less vigilant it could easily have been me awaiting burial in the small cemetery at my back. Had that been the case, however, with these tremendous views and the eternal prospect of the long downhill glide to the valley floor, it would be hard to find a more fitting resting place for a bicyclist.

The long thrilling descent into the Bierzo went on and on, the day becoming warmer and the countryside growing ever more fertile as I lost height. Around the charming village of Molinaseca the fields were white with the blossom of thousands of cherry trees brought there originally from the Black Sea coast of Turkey by the Romans who colonised this valley. I paused just long enough to see the famous bridge which had replaced the one which the turbulent Queen Urraca of Castile had demolished. The river had been dammed just below it and a splendid swimming place created. In warmer weather I would have stopped and swum there.

A short while later I was riding into the large sprawling town of Ponferrada which lies at the confluence of the Rivers Sil and Boeza. Once I had managed to wriggle a way through the bewildering industrial outskirts of this city (designed purely, it seemed, to confuse travellers) I was in a small and pretty old town relaxing in its late Sunday morning inactivity.

The oldest monuments in Ponferrada are two medieval

bridges spanning the deep river gorges. One of these was built in iron, so unusual a choice of material for the twelfth century that it gave the town its name. The most striking relic of the place, however, is the splendid thirteenth-century castle which was the Spanish headquarters of the Knights Templar. The castle is largely ruined but still conveys a quality of adventure and high romance, particularly the sharply cut battlements and the refurbished and flag-bedecked gatehouse, with its wealth of crenellated turrets. Ferdinand II of León granted Ponferrada to the Knights Templar in 1185, in order that they might protect the pilgrims on their way to Santiago, as well as assisting in the Reconquest. By that time the Templars were the most powerful of the orders of chivalry, having had more than sixty years to prove themselves in the Crusades. With its strict hierarchical structure, its emphasis on high birth and its secret rituals and initiation ceremonies, it produced in its members a monastic degree of obedience and discipline and an almost fanatical loyalty to the Order. But the power and wealth that the Knights accumulated and the arrogance they developed towards outside interference made a clash with higher authority inevitable. In 1312 the Knights Templar were expelled from Spain, and all over Europe and in England the Order was forcibly disbanded and their property confiscated. Present-day reminders of their considerable presence in medieval London are the Inns of Court and the Temple Church. Disbanded, the Knights Templar became idealised models for romantic tales of medieval chivalry and for the songs of the troubadours, just as Charlemagne and his paladins had before them.

The Templars had also founded the fine parish church of Nuestra Señora de la Encina. But like much of the centre of Ponferrada, this building had been largely reconstructed in the late sixteenth century and given a tall ornate Baroque bell tower. A sizeable congregation was just leaving the church as I arrived, and although once again I was sorry to have missed a Sunday service, I was able to add the stamp of the place to my pilgrim passport. It was a nice seal, celebrating the twelfth-century miracle of the Virgin and Child appearing to the populace in an oak tree.

A very neat grid system of streets stands next to the old part of Ponferrada and it was here I sought a much needed lunch – though actually the hearty midday meal I had grown accustomed to eating in Spain should more properly be called luncheon. It was the best compromise I had found for coping with the impossibly late Spanish evening meal, usually not served until I was in bed and asleep. After the splendid *menú del día* I needed only a light evening snack, and I could either get my own in the *refugio* or eat *tapas* in a bar. Breakfast could be a problem as nothing happened much before nine-thirty a.m. in Spain, so I needed to buy provisions the day before in order to get my own. Cycling after a heavy meal is not advisable, but as the Spanish luncheon was also served late, and I started my day very early, I often did not need to go on afterwards.

Neither luncheon, nor even a humble lunch proved easy to find in this part of Ponferrada on a Sunday, however, and after quartering the checker board streets for a considerable time, I thought I had better settle for the 'Ho Cheng'. It is usually interesting to see how Chinese food changes its image according to the taste of the host country. But after satisfying the worst of my hunger at this place I was not surprised that I was their only customer. The amount I had managed to eat would certainly not inconvenience me on the uphill road to Villafranca del Bierzo.

All the pilgrims I spoke to afterwards found the route

out of Ponferrada one of the most confusing parts of their journey. I was no exception. I added several extra miles to my route and practised my Spanish assiduously in attempts to enlist local help in getting me back on the *Camino*, but it seemed a very long time before I was free of the confusion of major roads. And even when I thought I was finally established on my correct way to Villafranca del Bierzo, a passer-by spotting my shells had to redirect me to another road. Once I was truly launched it proved a pleasant ride in warm sunshine through the vineyards of the Bierzo.

Just before descending to the town of Villafranca del Bierzo the pilgrim comes to one of the most significant and evocative places of the pilgrimage. The austerely beautiful little Romanesque church of Santiago looks much as it must have done for the best part of a thousand years, standing at the side of the rough track, with below it the first glimpse of the town in its pleasant valley, with the green hills beyond. It is a simple single-apsed church of quiet dignity. All its ornamentation is concentrated around a rich portal in the northern wall of the nave, a door known as the Puerta del Perdón. Pilgrims who had managed to make their way as far as this 'Doorway of Pardon', and who were too sick to go any further, could claim the same absolution as if they had reached the shrine of St James itself. It would have been surprising if so revered a spot had not retained its atmosphere and I sat there, quite alone, for a long time gazing down on the attractive little town below, cradled among the green hills.

Villafranca, as its name suggests, was more French than Spanish, having been founded and managed by Cluny at a time when establishing towns along the threatened remnant of Christian Spain was as important as the pilgrimage itself. Suitable Christian settlers were not all that easy to attract, so likely ones were sometimes deflected from their pilgrimage and persuaded to ply their various skills and trades in these new centres by promises of indulgences. Whether this happened in Villafranca or not I don't know, but for a poor man, or one with little land at home, this French town in its rich valley would be a tempting proposition. And however it attracted its original population, Villafranca quickly became a prosperous centre of trade and agriculture and is today one of the most attractive towns on the *Camino Francés*.

The Benedictines of Cluny were joined here by the Jesuits and the Franciscans, and all three orders built splendid churches in the town, so there were many fine monuments to visit. Villafranca's chief delight for me, however, apart from the relaxed spacious feel of the place, was the narrow Calle del Agua, which ran down to the pleasant river and was lined with imposing sixteenth- and seventeenth-century merchants' houses, flamboyant coats of arms prominently displayed.

There was no *refugio* in Villafranca, other than a plastic tent beside the church of Santiago. I thought of staying in the Hotel Commercio, a delightful period piece which made me think I had been transported back to pre-revolution France. It was a cavernous place, and what paint there was on doors and window frames was that particular shade of grey which could only be French. The scores of small bedrooms had bare scrubbed boards two or three feet wide and little iron bedsteads. There was one shower for what could have amounted to well over a hundred guests, and this was clearly a later addition – though as dated as it was possible for it to be and still remain functional. The dining room almost defied description so antique and darkly atmospheric was it, the brown walls hung with blackened pictures and barely room to squeeze between the crowded tables. But it was not a place to enjoy alone I decided, and suddenly I remembered my own small tent, and thought of it set among the green meadows I had seen across the valley.

That evening was perfect for camping, clear and bright and not nearly so cold as it had been of late. I found a spot not far out of town where the landscape was probably very little different from what the medieval pilgrims had seen. Roberts had been manhandled up and along a steep little footpath until there was not a house in sight and I pitched the tent in a spot thick with wild flowers. Since I felt my body needed to recover from the dubious lunch, I made do without an evening meal and doctored myself with a small hot whisky instead, a sovereign remedy for most ills.

It was lovely to be in the tent again with the doors fastened back so that I could see the stars. Santiago pilgrims must have spent many such nights in the open, wrapped in their cloaks looking up at these same skies. Aimery Picaud divides the way from the Pyrenees into thirteen stages, but even with a stout horse it is extremely doubtful that the distance – anything from 440 to 500 miles (and even more with detours) – could have been covered in even twice as many days. On foot it would have been impossible to do it in less than four weeks. Monasteries and hospices were often far apart, nor were there sufficient places in them to ensure every pilgrim could shelter for each night of his journey. On many nights they must have slept rough. I felt very much at one with them here, on the old pilgrim track above Villafranca, especially I think, because of the sense of trust in a beneficent God that always seems to go with sleeping without the protection of walls.

I got going early next day, in spite of the extra chore of striking camp. It was as well that I did so, for the next stretch of the *Camino* goes through the narrow cleft of the beautiful Valcarce where, for the first ten miles or so, there is little opportunity of avoiding the N VI. Only a few short detours offer all too brief respites from this murderously fast road. But what respites! The moment I left the bare hot strip of tarmac I would be plunged into lanes darkly shadowed by trees, where picturesque old villages gave way to hedgerows thick with broom, primroses, wild hellebore, speedwell, campion, hawthorn, grass of parnassus, iris, dog violets, apple blossom and scores of other growing things I failed to record. None of these escape routes lasted long, they simply served to remind me constantly of how lovely life could be without the addition of trunk roads.

Not until Ambasmestas where the new N VI takes off on the first of a series of spectacular giant viaducts can the cyclist finally escape. The old N VI follows a less spectacular course, though infinitely more beautiful, climbing, plunging and twisting through the gorges of the Cordillera Cantábrica. Several times the new road crosses the old one, sailing above it at what seemed like an impossible height. But stiff climbing though it was on my road at times, not for a moment did I envy the rushing vehicles their high wire of a road: from where I was it looked terrifying. Very little traffic passed me on my way, and I was able to enjoy my ride in peace and tranquillity (just as the 'Pilgrim's Itinerarium' hoped I would). In a surprisingly short time, so fit was I by now, I had crossed into Galicia on the last stages of my journey. Pointing Roberts even more steeply upwards I began the climb to the ancient sanctuary of O Cebreiro, the legendary resting place of the Holy Grail.

13

Regions of Mist and Legend

As I toiled up the steep winding road out of the chestnut woods, a valley opened up far below me to the right, a patchwork of small fields, all neatly divided by grey granite walls, its vibrant and infinite variety of green was astonishing. Under the blue, rain-washed sky with its dusting of white cloud, the Galician landscape had a freshness about it that put energy into my tired muscles, and made me think that the best of the journey had been kept for the final stages. Nor was I alone in this thought; Aimery Picaud's guide also waxes lyrical over Galicia.

'. . . a well watered region with rivers and meadows and fine orchards, excellent fruit and clear springs . . .'

And with his customary strong xenophobic bias, he bestows on the people of the region the ultimate accolade:

'The Galicians are more like our French people in their customs than any other of the uncultivated races of Spain.'

The journey had presented such a wealth of variety that I would have expected it to have exhausted its repertoire by now. Yet here I was, almost at the end of the eleventh of Aimery Picaud's thirteen stages, with less than a hundred miles to go to Santiago, and once again I was in a region that both looked and felt delightfully different. This difference was expressed in every line, shade and aspect of the countryside, but as I came over the brow of the hill I saw that the works of man were even more novel.

Perched on its small plateau among a panorama of hills was the little hamlet of O Cebreiro, with its strange stone-age *pallozas*, surely the most extraordinary dwellings to have survived into the twentieth century. Round, or rather oval in shape, they have low thick walls and a curious thatched roof that rises to a single point, though never quite over the precise centre of the building. The traditional houses of Galicia – and no two are ever quite alike – vary to suit the pitch and lay of the ground they are built upon. Sometimes they are tucked into the side of a hill so that one flank of the building is below ground. Traditionally they were shared by the cows and other livestock, and were built with a decided slope towards the animals' half so that drainage should be in their direction. Inside, a simple half wall divided the two apartments, leaving the greater share for the humans. An open hearth with no chimney, one or two very small windows and an enormous central kingpost to support the roof, and you had a home that could defy the worst that wind and weather could hurl at it. That it would also be smoky and certainly dark were small considerations to a hardy outdoor people. With regional variations, such habitations once existed all over the Celtic West, though none was as distinctive as these in Galicia, nor have any others remained in use for quite so long, except perhaps the 'black houses' of the Hebrides. In Cebreiro a few of these *pallozas* are still in use, though I believe they are no longer shared by the livestock. As I stood there admiring them I had no idea I was to spend the night in one.

Satisfyingly strange and attractive though I found them, however, there would be *pallozas* in other places, while there was nowhere else on the entire route that had the unique attraction of Cebreiro's church, and it was to this building that I now made my way.

A Benedictine monastery and a pilgrim hospice had been founded at Cebreiro as early as the ninth century, though it seems likely that the place had already acquired a special significance. At some point it became one of the rumoured resting places of the Holy Grail, and although scholars have advanced a score of different reasons for it, no one knows how or why this came about. The legend of the Holy Grail (the cup or chalice which Christ had used at the Last Supper) is one of the most mystical traditions to have arisen out of the relic cult and it was one that exerted a tremendous hold on the Christian imagination. The basis of the belief was that Joseph of Arimathea preserved the chalice, together with a few drops of the blood from Christ's pierced side, and sailed away with it to seek a place of safe keeping. There are tales of the Holy Grail appearing in almost as many different sites as the wood of the True Cross, but the accounts are particularly concentrated in the Celtic West. Medieval romances, like the Arthurian legends, have the 'Quest for the Holy Grail' as their central theme, the ultimate prize which can be won only by the 'perfect knight' without stain or blemish.

An echo of the ardent and mystical beliefs surrounding the Holy Grail occurred again at Cebreiro in the thirteenth century, when the church became the celebrated site of a miracle. One bitter winter's day a peasant had trudged far through the snow to hear mass, the only person to have braved the fearful weather. The officiating priest had sneered at him for making such an effort 'just for a bit of bread and wine'. At this, the story goes, the elements became the actual body and blood of Christ, and a wooden statue of the Virgin on the adjacent wall turned her head towards the altar to witness the event. The miracle established Cebreiro as a site of pilgrimage in its own right, one of the most significant stops on the way to Santiago.

With all these tales of miracles and romance in my mind I came to the walled enclosure at the top of the village with the glebe field behind and the two small dark slate buildings. Even though I knew that both structures had been almost entirely rebuilt, my first thought was how ancient and absolutely right they looked with their dry-stone walling and simple dignity.

The monastery had begun to decline by the seventeenth century, and by 1960, when Don Elías Valiña, a local priest devoted to the pilgrimage, had started the work of restoration, the place was almost in ruins. What is there now is a great testimony to his efforts. The little hostelry has become a simple hotel, an unpretentious place with a log fire, long tables and benches, delightfully in keeping with the pilgrimage.

The church gives no hint of being rebuilt, and most authorities claim that the design can have changed little, if at all, from the original ninth-century structure. It is a modest three-aisled building, almost square, with a sturdy bell tower at one corner, the bells exposed in simple Romanesque arches. The interior walls have been left bare except for a statue of the Virgin – whether it was the very one whose head had turned in reverence I did not know. Nearby in a glass case is the twelfth-century chalice and patten, together with a reliquary for holding the preserved bread and wine of the famous miracle, given by King Ferdinand and Queen Isabella when they came here on pilgrimage in 1486. There was a story that the royal couple had intended to take the divine elements with them, but they refused to be moved.

The chalice is exquisite, a masterpiece of the goldsmith's art. But over and above the beauty of the vessels there is no doubt that the church gains an extra dimension by having them there, a visible link with their past. The objects themselves would also lose much of their sense of wonder in a museum. In Cebreiro's little church, where Arthurian legend has so closely woven itself into the Christian story, there is something very special, and certainly nowhere is more evocative of the age of medieval pilgrimage.

If I wanted to spend the night at Cebreiro, and I most certainly did, I had the choice of my tent or one of the *pallozas* that served as a *refugio*. I chose the latter without hesitation, but was able, by special favour, to have a much-needed bath in the hotel before the luxury of an evening meal. Most of the four or five rooms there had been reserved for Spanish men who were working on the electricity supply of the hamlet, and who lived too far away to go home at night. The only remaining room had been taken by Guy and Michèle, a young French couple who were also on their way to Santiago by car and whom I had already met in the church. They invited me to share their table so that we could talk about the journey. Guy taught history at a Paris school and Michèle worked in a bookshop, and neither had known much about the pilgrimage before setting out – but already they had decided that the car was no way to see it properly, and were determined to do part of it again in the summer by bicycle. I could see Michèle giving me occasional surreptitious glances, and I imagined her thinking, 'If she can do it at her age, I certainly can,' a thought I did my best to encourage.

The meal was roast pig and chips, which was a speciality of the region – the pig anyway – and quite delicious, and with it we drank what was probably a local wine, though as it came in a jug rather than a bottle we couldn't tell. The local men were drinking cider. It was so late by the time the pudding of *crème caramel* (the national dish of Spain, I think, since I had it at nearly every meal) was eaten and the wine was finished that I thought I had better forego coffee in the interests of sleep, and take a little walk to shake down the rich food.

When I went outside, however, I found it was already dark, and raining lightly also, so I made for my *palloza* instead, armed with candles and torch. Roberts was to share it with me so I would be reverting to dual occupancy of a sort. As I passed between the other *pallozas*, an elderly woman came out of one and said something to me in Spanish which I did not understand, but as she accompanied her words with gestures of eating I realised she was offering me food. I was able to thank her for the offer in Spanish, but I too had to resort to mime to convey the information that I had eaten already. She would not let me go, however, before she had pressed a couple of tiny apples into my hand. I had only caught a limited view into the yellow-lit interior behind her, just enough to gain a vague impression of cosiness, a refuge from the dark wet night. I wished afterwards that I had been able to ask to see how it was furnished.

My *palloza* looked enormous by flickering candlelight,

with the rough beams supporting the thatch high above my head lost, like Roberts, among the shadows. There was nothing at all in the place other than the straw strewn over the stone floor. It was like a rustic hall of unknown antiquity, and very cold – which was small wonder since Cebreiro stands at around the 1300-metre mark. The straw rustled with movements other than mine, but I had wrapped the tent snugly around my sleeping bag and felt reasonably secure from rats: mice I don't really mind, and anyway I would have put up with a lot worse for the adventure of sleeping in this stone-age refuge. I propped myself up on my elbow for a while to read the enormous pilgrims' logbook. As usual there were entries in many languages. Most of what I could read spoke in some sense of 'finding the real *Camino* in this place', a sentiment I shared.

As I pulled the coverings tightly around me and prepared for sleep, I wondered if the rain would persist and obliterate this, my third and final mountain range of the journey, as had happened with the other two. Galicia is often referred to as 'the land of the umbrella' so it was with some trepidation that I poked my head out of the *palloza* as soon as I awoke the following morning. The skies were not only clear, but flushed so softly with a suggestion of pink and gold that it was like the subtle wash in a Japanese print. I pulled on my clothes quickly and went out for a wider view. Around the back of the village past the church and the granite cross, the ground falls away sharply from the road and a range of hills spreads out as far as the eye can see. The valleys were filled with mist and each range of hills was no more than a dark brushstroke. The sun was somewhere behind the mist, invisible, but adding a faint translucence so that the scene appeared quite unearthly and wildly beautiful. I thought as I gazed at it, that it was as close to a vision of heaven as I was likely to see in this life.

There was a moment almost as wonderful a few hours later as I came over the 1327-metre peak of Santa Maria del Poyo to a fresh panorama of hills and wooded valleys, basking in golden sunshine and spreading westward as far as the eye could see. After the first exhilarating descent summit followed summit, and it would have been hard work had I not stopped often to take in this wholly delightful corner of Spain. The rain-washed countryside was reminiscent of Wales and Cornwall and wonderfully restful after the arid regions of Castile. But while Galicia recalled other Celtic lands it was quite different from any of them. Even the fine granite crosses bearing their sturdy figures of Christ, which were a feature of the region, were nothing like the tall crosses of Ireland and Western Scotland with their intricate interwoven patterning. Galician patterns where they occurred were geometric and angular.

A frequent and particularly entertaining feature of the landscape were the *hórreos*. Had I not seen something vaguely similar in Central Africa I might have thought the Galicians buried their dead in elaborate small tombs raised on tall pillars, as the ancient Lycians had done, particularly as the miniature pitched roofs were finished off with crosses and various ornamentation. But the elaborate little structures were storage chambers, and the pillars were padstones to prevent rats getting at the grain.

The fields tended to be small, very neat and well cared for, and like everything else in the countryside had a delightfully old-fashioned look about them. As for the villages and small hamlets, with their *pallozas*, *hórreos* and other venerable stone houses and churches, they seemed caught in a time warp. It was small wonder that I made only very slow progress westward that day.

The idyll continued until I found I was sharing the road with imperious trucks that belted along at a furious rate, coating everything around them with a fine dust. I thought at first they were carrying loose cement, but then I remembered reading in Aimery Picaud's guide that medieval pilgrims had taken large stones from near Tricastela and carried them five leagues to where they were made into lime for the building of the new cathedral at Santiago. After that the nuisance of the trucks was tempered by the thought that I might be witnessing the continuation of one of the longest running businesses in history.

By mid-afternoon, with all the many stops, I had made only twenty-five miles when I halted in the small village of Samos outside the charming baroque façade of a simply enormous monastery. I was about to ring the bell and see if I could have a quick look at the place when a monk in the habit of a Benedictine popped his head round the door and beckoned me in. It was exactly as though he had been expecting me, and without preamble began to lead me around on a tour of the cloisters.

The elaborate complex took up most of the wooded valley, which in consequence seemed much larger from inside the walls than from outside. It was one of the oldest Benedictine foundations in Spain predating the finding of the body of St James by at least three hundred years. When the Moors overran the area in the eighth century it had been abandoned, and was revived again when they had retreated in the ninth.

The present vast place was begun in the twelfth century, but it had burnt down so often that it is all a bit of a mish mash now, with some strange statuary, especially one of large bare-breasted females cavorting in a fountain, not usually the sort of thing associated with monasteries. The entire top floor around the great cloister, replaced only a few decades ago after yet another disastrous fire, was decorated with a series of the most awful modern paintings showing the life of St Benedict. In fact, apart from the charming exterior façade, which was the west wall of the church, I can't say I liked any of it very much, but as the monk enthusiastically led me on I wasn't able to escape. The interior of the enormous barrel-vaulted, eighteenth-century church particularly depressed me. It appeared to be entirely without windows and so still and airless that, huge and rich as it was, it seemed like a tomb, and a sudden surge of claustrophobia made me beat a hasty retreat back to the fresh air.

It transpired that my tour had been the result of mistaken identity. Part of the monastery operates an hotel now and the monk had been expecting a group of people and thought I was in advance of the main party. The coach carrying these guests arrived just as I was trying to make my escape, and so I was left to discover the most enchanting monument in Samos on my own. The site of the original monastery lies outside the walls of the present complex, hidden in a small muddy copse. There was nothing to indicate its whereabouts, nor did I quite know what to expect. I thought I had gone the wrong way, until, suddenly, I came upon it, a tiny and wonderfully primitive slate chapel dwarfed by massive pines, one of which pressed so closely against it that it would seem to threaten the fabric. There was such a sense of antiquity about this homely little building and – as at Cebreiro – such a sense of rightness that it was hard to believe it had any connection with the grandiose pile which had supplanted it.

I had been thinking of spending the night at the monastery's *refugio* but now I decided to push on another eight miles to the town of Sarria. This proved a happy choice. The old town, which was an important pilgrim centre in medieval times, is a quiet backwater now perched on top of a hill. Although nothing much remained there of architectural merit, the place was redolent of the pilgrimage with its castle ruins and acres of quiet semi-rural decay in which stood a small Romanesque church and the former hospital and monastery of La Madalena still offering a shelter to pilgrims.

Climbing up to it I passed a small antique building which was being restored, and when I stopped to look more closely was much amused to read on the plaque that it had been a jail where reprobate pilgrims were locked up.

A small girl accompanied me for the last few hundred yards after I had stopped to ask her where I could find the *refugio*. She was a competent child of about eight or nine who absolutely refused to accept that my Spanish was as bad as I claimed. With admirable perseverance she succeeded in getting me to understand that her brother went to the school next door to the monastery, and that he played football with one of the brothers. I think she was glad of the opportunity to visit this male sanctum and insisted on bringing me right to the door; even ringing the bell and waiting to explain to whoever opened it that I was a pilgrim. Perhaps she had done it all before as the brother who came to the door seemed less charmed by her than I had been and sent her on her way quite curtly.

It was a very simple *refugio*, just one large room which was already occupied by three French families with some fourteen children between them, all under ten, and most of them scurrying around like small demons. But though this might sound rather daunting, and certainly seemed so at first, it proved a most entertaining evening. The three families were friends who were doing the pilgrimage by degrees; a certain amount each holiday. They had taken two years over it and were now on the final stage. At least two of the youngest offspring had been born since the start of the venture. But just like the pilgrims carved on the door at Burgos, they had not let babes-in-arms change their plans.

Each family had an old, workman-like van packed tight with bedding, cooking gear, stores and clothing. Their method of travel was that as many as could – or wanted to – walked, while the adults took it in turns to drive the vehicles and to meet the walkers at places where the routes merged. Sometimes, they told me, they would drive back and forth several times over a stretch so that everyone had their chance of walking it.

The children all kept scrap books and diaries, and recorded their impressions in words or pictures as they went along. Later, when I wrote up my notes, they let me see their books and I thought that between them they had put together an impressive body of knowledge. St James, or *St Jacques* as he was to them, came out of it very well in illustrations as amusing as only young children's drawings can be before they become self-conscious about them.

The parents were impressive too. The organisation nec-essary for such a trip, the hundred and one things to consider for so many, was fearsome. All the time I had been talking with the children, the six adults had been hard at work cooking, washing clothes, tending to babies, answering questions and doing the hundred and one things parents have to do anywhere, but with infinitely more difficulty because of coping with such primitive conditions.

I was invited to share their supper of macaroni, salad, fruit and wine, but was not permitted to help wash up in return because of them having their own routine. Instead I had the decidedly more pleasurable task of holding dear, placid, little baby Henri, while his mother wielded a dish cloth. Afterwards, when the tremendous activity of getting fourteen children washed and ready for bed began, I retired to my tent in a green field behind the monastery, happy to have seen and shared for a while yet another dimension of pilgrimage. The day ended beautifully with a sky full of swallows swooping and darting low over the meadow, while from all sides came the distant lowing of cattle.

And that was the end of my period of pleasant contentment for a while, because after Sarria came a very dreary and heavy bit of the pilgrimage. The weather did not help; I had woken to a grey overcast day that drained the landscape of its magic. The town of Puertomarín depressed me still further. It was a small town that had been built to replace an ancient one, sacrificed some years before to the building of a dam on the River Miño and lying now beneath the waters of the newly created lake. Like all such re-sited towns, the sense of its upheaval still hung over it, giving it a melancholy air. It appeared to be rootless. Nowhere was this more apparent than in its large fortress-like Romanesque church which had been moved stone by stone to this present site. The great Abu Simbel temple in Upper Egypt, re-sited at a cost of billions of dollars after the building of the Aswan Dam, has much the same feeling of the spirit of the place having fled elsewhere.

Standing there in this stripped-down church, I felt that all connection with the pilgrimage had vanished. The journey had lost its momentum and suddenly I wanted desperately for it to come to an end. There and then I decided to push on to Santiago. I had, I felt, to get there today; another night would be too much.

This was easier said than done, for the terrain seemed designed expressly to defeat haste. The hills never let up and it began to seem like the hardest day's cycling of the whole journey. Under a cold grey drizzle I began to notice the discarded rubbish lying along the verges and in the hedges more than the pretty sloping fields with their neat slate walls.

It became even less pleasurable once the route led me back to the main roads and the callous speeding traffic. Bunyan would have approved I thought grimly: there had obviously been altogether too much enjoyment in this pilgrimage and not nearly enough struggle. Now the only thing left was to grit the teeth and concentrate on the cycling.

I had a temporary respite from this bleak period when I made the short detour to the isolated Romanesque church of Vilar de Donas, against whose damp interior walls, bright green with mould, stand some of the fine funereal effigies of the Knights of Santiago. There were also some lovely frescoes of the Annunciation and the Resurrection still glowing on the walls of the apse in spite of the damp. The whole building was rather stunning in fact, standing there miles from anywhere on a pitted and ruinous little country road, and it cheered me up no end.

But there was nothing else of architectural merit to make me pause in any of the towns now until Santiago itself. I only stopped at Melide because I could not continue without a meal, having covered forty-eight miles since striking camp that morning. I had a further thirty-five to do if I was to make Santiago that day.

I met a Belgian pilgrim in Melide, a walker who was also

having a bad day. The walkers' track, he told me, was in an awful state; he had not had dry feet since he could remember. He thought he would need three more days to reach Santiago, but hoped to do it in two. Listening to the resignation and tiredness in his voice I realised again how much harder is the pilgrimage for walkers, how endless the bleak featureless stretches like this one must seem. Perhaps even Harrie might feel some sense of urgency at this stage, and a desire for journey's end.

After a good sustaining meal of bean stew and *tortilla* I walked for a while through Melide's streets to allow the food to settle before cycling on, and somewhere between the two locked Romanesque churches I caught the unmistakable skirl of bagpipes, a lovely and stirring sound to those who, like me, enjoy it. I tracked it to a house that opened straight onto the pavement, and was listening entranced when the window flew up and the musicians urged me to come inside.

They settled me in a deep armchair, a glass of wine in my hand, and for ten minutes or so I was treated to an impromptu concert of Galician music. The pipes were not unlike Scottish pipes except that the drones were arranged differently and the sound, I thought, was not quite so resonant – which was just as well – with three pipers playing away with gusto in a small room, together with a drummer. If I could have chosen anything I liked to cheer me up, I probably wouldn't have thought of a trio of Galician pipers, but it was exactly what was needed, and I remembered to thank St Raphael, as well as the musicians.

No sooner was I outside than the rain came on again, strongly enough to don full rain gear and to tie plastic bags over my only shoes. Then it was once more, head down, ignore the aching muscles and the trickle of rain down the neck, and cycle on.

As the hills became less steep so the landscape grew steadily uglier and more industrialised. Even when the rain slackened to a thin drizzle it looked little better. I cycled on, very tired by this time; too tired in fact to think of anything, except perhaps an end to the effort, when suddenly out of nowhere came a warm glow of happiness at the realisation that I was approaching Santiago.

Up to this moment I had not given much thought to arriving. The journey had absorbed all my interest and I hadn't needed to look forward. But now in the middle of this last unattractive stretch Santiago assumed a reality. It was no longer just the town at the journey's end, but the goal to which I had been heading all these weeks, a special and holy place. At the same time I again had the sense of St James at my shoulder pushing me on over the last stages. I passed Labacolla, where the pilgrims had performed their ritual ablutions before coming into sight of the city. But this is now the site of Santiago's airport and offers little to tempt a pilgrim to stop. Over a shoulder of Monte de Gozo I climbed. Somewhere to my right was the knoll, the *Montjoie* from which traditionally the towers of the cathedral of Santiago can first be seen, though not on such a day as this I decided, and sped on.

The evening traffic was thick as I came to the outskirts of Santiago. The high-rise blocks and a bewildering complexity of roads, every one of which seemed to be in the process of being rebuilt, extended for what seemed a very long way. All my attention was needed for survival; the route finding I left to St James. Amid all the depressing ugliness of the approach I caught sight for a moment of one small gem, the medieval chapel of St Lazarus. It gave me a foretaste of wonders to come and the courage to continue through the maelstrom of the traffic. And then, quite suddenly the effort was all over.

There are no medieval walls or gateways to mark the entry to this superlatively beautiful city. The noisy bustling traffic simply ceases at the point where the medieval city begins, and only very few vehicles venture through its paved and winding roads. Buildings of several different periods line the quiet alleyways, particularly masterpieces of the Baroque and the Renaissance. But it is the genius of the Middle Ages which underpins and illuminates the whole structure of the city of Santiago. All roads here lead naturally to the shrine of St James, the focus and inspiration of the journey.

14

Santiago de Compostela

The end of a lengthy journey is always an emotional experience. Either the arrival has been so longingly anticipated
that it must prove something of a disappointment, or
the journey itself has been so idyllic that its ending is
unwelcome. Either way, few destinations entirely live up
to a traveller's expectations.

This particular journey, however, was like no other I
had ever undertaken. For, although there had been so
many highlights of architecture, landscape and experience
and so many rich encounters with people and places along
the way that it would be extraordinary if Santiago did not
prove something of an anti-climax, once I had stepped
over the invisible barrier where the medieval walls once
girded the city, there was never any danger that it would.
As I wheeled Roberts down the paved arcaded streets of
Santiago, I realised with delight that, just as crossing into
Galicia had seemed like keeping the best of the journey until
last, so this city was undoubtedly the jewel in its crown, a
conviction which grew with every step.

Santiago is built of a warm brownish granite that comes
alive in the rain. Still wet from the recent downpour,

the mica in the stone sparkled from every magnificent Baroque façade. I had not expected this Baroque elegance in what I had thought of as essentially a medieval city. But of course, nothing could be more natural. As the flow of pilgrims had swelled the cathedral coffers, so the city had continued to expand, and to add to and embellish its many churches and monasteries. Happily the greatest spate of rebuilding had been in the seventeenth and early eighteenth centuries when Spanish architecture was superb; and the decline in pilgrimage, which began soon afterwards, resulted in Santiago being preserved at its peak. Nevertheless it is a medieval city both in its layout and in its underlying structure. And, as I was soon to discover, the great Romanesque buildings are still to be found within their Baroque or Renaissance shells.

But that sort of exploration would come later. What struck me immediately was the atmosphere. Here was no dead showpiece of a city, as many historic towns have become, but a place bustling with everyday life. Being a university city means that the streets are thronged with students as well as with foreign visitors, and townspeople go about their everyday affairs among them as they have always done. Santiago has a thousand-year-old tradition of accommodating large numbers of people, from kings to beggars, and this had clearly not been lost.

There was none of the usual tourist tat to be seen either: the souvenir shops with their horrible stocks of cheap kitsch did not seem to exist. What was on display in Santiago seemed largely to come from Galicia itself, and to have a practical purpose. Restaurants were particularly numerous, their windows displaying such wonders as large octopuses boiled whole, mounds of St James' own queen scallops, lobsters, crabs, oysters, and scores of other edible molluscs

I had never seen before. Shops selling all manner of cheeses were also common – again there was an extraordinary range including ones shaped liked women's breasts. Bookshops existed side by side with hotels, music shops, haberdashers and greengrocers. Shops catering expressly for tourists were those plying ancient trades in their traditional sites around the cathedral, like the jewellery workers in jet, the goldsmiths and the silversmiths.

Everywhere there were sights to distract and divert a pilgrim from the traditional route. Even modern troubadours, usually students, sent up their beguiling threads of sounds from bagpipes, clarinets and fiddles under the shelter of the arcades. And because there was only foot traffic and the occasional bicycle in the flagstoned streets and alleys, there was the opportunity to stop and gaze without having to leap for safety every other minute.

So altogether it was small wonder that I felt I had plunged into the world of the Middle Ages as soon as I entered Santiago, and was tempted to stand and gawp like any country bumpkin at a hundred and one new wonders. But as all roads in a great medieval city radiate outwards from its heart, so everyone who enters its mesh will eventually be drawn to its true centre. Wander as aimlessly as you will in Santiago, sooner or later you emerge into the stunning magnificence of the Plaza del Obradoiro.

What was once the 'Field of the Star' is now one of the noblest squares in Europe, and there are few people who do not catch their breath in astonishment at their first sight of it. The wide uninterrupted space spreads out in front of the soaring extravagance of the west wall of the cathedral, the Obradoiro façade – a name meaning 'work in gold' that has also been given to the plaza. Three other fine buildings flank the remaining sides, but it is the towering portico added to the Romanesque cathedral in the eighteenth century which needs every foot of the plaza to be appreciated in its full splendour.

Santiago is not built on level ground, and the Plaza del Obradoiro is about twenty feet below the level of the cathedral floor, so there is already the sense of great elevation. A heavy double stone staircase ascends from the square to the west door, and above that a rich profusion of statuary and decoration mounts upwards, tier upon tier, to culminate in two immensely tall elaborate bell towers flanking an intricate gable, at the apex of which a statue of Santiago Peregrino is enshrined in an arch. It is Spanish Baroque at its most exuberant, and it works because the sheer extravagance of ornamentation has been balanced with architectural integrity. The result is a triumph, especially as the granite is warmed by red and yellow lichens that flourish in the warm wet climate. Very little of this wealth of detail was apparent to me on this first visit, however. There was an order to be observed in arriving at Santiago, and the time for leisurely sight-seeing would come later.

The ritual that the modern pilgrim observes has been followed for as long as the cathedral has stood here. Having mounted the flights of stairs from the square and passed through the Obradoiro façade, I was face to face with the Pórtico de la Gloria and the actual world of the medieval pilgrim. The lively and exuberant had been replaced by the sublime. A Master Mateo carved and signed this 'Gate of Glory', the original western façade of the Romanesque cathedral, in 1188, and what strikes one about it at first glance is the expression of exalted serenity on the faces of the vast array of figures – Christ, St James, the twenty-four elders, apostles and prophets. The whole company of the

Heavenly Host are assembled here, as though the pilgrims have arrived at the actual Gate of Glory where St Peter stands, key in hand, to let them in. The tragedy of the Obradoiro façade, lovely as it is, is that you cannot step back and see this Pórtico de la Gloria in its entirety as could the medieval pilgrim.

The central pillar of the immense carving is a Tree of Jesse tracing the ancestry of Christ from Adam, and near the base the alabaster has been worn into deep grooves into which the fingers and thumb of the right hand slip naturally as each pilgrim in turn bows the head and recites the prayers of thankfulness for safe arrival. As the head bends so Master Mateo comes into view crouched at the base of his work.

Once past the threshold the perfect proportions of the twelfth-century building are revealed, just as Aimery Picaud saw them:

'In this church there is no defect; it is admirably built, large and spacious, clear, of fitting size, harmoniously proportioned in breadth, length, and height; and it is of two storeys, like a royal palace. If a man is sorrowful and he goes up into the galleries, he will be happy and comforted after contemplating its perfect beauty.'

At the head of the long uninterrupted view up through the austerely simple nave and beyond the transept is a blaze of gold where the high altar stands. Beneath lie the relics of St James, and above is a thirteenth-century statue of him encased in metal, with a gem-encrusted metal cloak. The huge canopy over the altar is supported by bizarre outsized angels of doubtful lineage. But what the newly arrived pilgrims see, exalted as they are at the end of their long trek and by all the magnificence and beauty they have already seen in the approach to their goal, is the pool of warm golden light drawing them on.

As I set off up the nave I did not think it strange to feel myself one of a large band, a veritable army in fact. They were all around me as they had been throughout the journey, but it was in these moments that I was most aware of them. Narrow steps lead up behind the altar, and each pilgrim in turn embraces the statue of St James from behind. Awkward though it seemed, there was nothing unnatural about it; I felt I knew something of St James after this long journey.

Down the steps on the other side, turn left and left again down more narrow steps. Here in the small space beneath the altar is an embossed silver casket holding whatever remains of the bones which for eleven hundred years and more have been revered as those of St James. This was the spot where all those who had asked me to pray for them would wish me to do so, and as there was a bench I sat and read the names from my notebook. It took a long while because often I thought about the person as I read the name, and sometimes it was not like prayer at all but simple reminiscence, a reliving of the journey.

I wondered how the medieval pilgrims faced the same task. We would use virtually the same words but no doubt mean different things by them. Nor had I changed my mind about the likelihood of the remains of St James being here in this silver casket. St James of the Gospels, the brother of John, son of Zebedee, disciple of Christ had nothing at all to do with this place as far as I was concerned, not in the corporeal sense anyway. The St James who was enshrined here, the St James I had gradually become aware of on the pilgrimage, was what had come from the hearts and minds of the thousands and thousands of people who had walked the

Camino de Santiago for all these hundreds of years, struggling with meanings, with conscience, with faith and with the lack of it. It was because of them that there was a *Camino*, and all I could hope to do was to add my prayers to theirs, just as I had added my stone to the pile at the foot of the cross at Foncebadón. Coming to the end of my list I could now go up the steps on the other side and set about enjoying this splendid place.

While I was waiting next day for the priest who would check my credentials and, if they proved worthy, award me my *Compostela*, a young man told me that I was lucky to be there on this day for I would see the *botafumeiro* swung at mass in a little while. This was indeed a piece of good fortune. Being so early in the season there were few special masses where this unique ritual took place. The *botafumeiro* is an enormous silver censer, so big and heavy that it is carried in on poles by two burly townsmen clad in dark red robes. Further red-robed acolytes let down a chain and pulley suspended from the centre of the transept and attached the censer to it by a rope as thick as an arm. Then, with the incense lit and smoking thickly, the *botafumeiro* is swung to and fro across the transept with all four men controlling the ropes. I had not anticipated the colossal great arc it would make – a hundredweight or more of gleaming metal sweeping backwards and forwards, nearly touching the ground before swinging up again almost to the ceiling, the incense rising in great obscuring clouds. With the blaze of gold from the great high altar behind, the scene had a wonderfully barbaric quality, like Rembrandt's huge painting of Belshazzar's Feast.

Much of Santiago seemed like that, tremendously special but without fuss; things simply happened around one without the need to make great efforts. I had booked into the small friendly Hotel Suso, a short stone's throw from the cathedral, where I had a tiny room high up under the eaves and Roberts was locked up somewhere out of harm's way. No one needed a bicycle in Santiago. For several days I wandered in and out of churches, palaces and monasteries, any one of which would have been a worthy expedition in its own right; and at least once a day I was in the cathedral. As with all such truly great buildings it could not be taken in all at once, but had to be absorbed slowly, with frequent breaks for refreshment in one of the many convenient little bars.

Just sitting on the steps of the cathedral looking out over the Obradoiro square was refreshing because of the view of the pleasant rural landscape beyond. Because the countryside was so plainly in sight I never had the oppressive sense of being hemmed in while in Santiago, often the case with other cities.

Within the confines of the medieval city there was also Santiago's market, another delight that repaid several visits. Under one roof was gathered the wealth of Galicia's land and coastline – fruit, vegetables, dairy produce, meat and fish – all in great abundance like an overflowing cornucopia, displayed with neatness and artistry. It was even better than the restaurant windows for studying the amazing variety of shellfish, the octopuses and the great range of fish. The restaurants that flanked the market were particularly good too, though so far I had not had a meal in Galicia that was not both good and reasonable; that was yet to come.

If Santiago presents a problem for the visitor it is its extraordinary abundance. Its architectural riches alone are so extensive that no one with less than a month to spend there can hope to do more than scratch the surface. There are details, like the marvellous tympanum over the door of a little church dedicated to St Felix, that you come upon purely by accident, because being only one of such numerous wonders, few guide books bother to point it out. But although I saw only a fraction it did not worry me as it usually would, because somehow one doesn't seem to worry in Santiago. The week I spent there was notable mostly for a feeling of happy contentment. Only one incident struck a very different note, though in the end this was probably the most important thing that happened to me in Santiago. It was the occasion of the free pilgrim meal.

A privilege to which my *Compostela* entitled me was dining at the imposing Reyes Católicos Hospital, now a super-luxury hotel in the Parador chain. In theory I could have up to three meals a day there for three days, entirely gratis. The reason for this generosity is lodged in history and tradition of course, like all things to do with the St James pilgrimage. In 1501 King Ferdinand and Queen Isabella commissioned a pilgrim hospital to be worthy of so holy a place. No expense was spared in the building of it and the result is one of Santiago's most celebrated and beautiful buildings. The Reyes Católicos flanks the south side of the Plaza del Obradoiro and is built around four lovely courtyards each named for one of the four apostles and each one a little different from the others. The long low plain façade which faces onto the Obradoiro is relieved by the most restrained and delicate plateresque decoration and makes a perfect foil for the exuberant west front of the cathedral.

The Reyes Católicos immediately acquired a reputation for excellent hospitality. Pilgrims were limited to a three-day stay, unless they were sick, in which case the best of medical care was lavished upon them. Declining pilgrim numbers led to the hospice being converted to use as a hospital for sick local people – a role quite in keeping with the founders' charitable intentions. Subsequently, however, following the Spanish vogue for turning historic buildings into luxury hotels, the Reyes Católicos has become a hotel for extremely well-heeled visitors, which seems a rather less justifiable function for a place built to meet the needs of pilgrims. The free meals which the Reyes Católicos offers to ten pilgrims a day is its last link with tradition and, I would have thought, not only fair, but worth every penny of its paltry cost as a useful tourist attraction.

For Harrie was quite right about pilgrims being a great attraction for tourists, I discovered, now that I was on foot. I had not thought I looked anything like a pilgrim; I had no staff, rucksack, or wide-brimmed hat. The only clue was the scallop shell on my barbag which I now carried as a shoulder bag. But as the priest who had made out my *Compostela* had said, 'You can always tell who are pilgrims, there is a look about them.' Weather-beaten I certainly was, but it seems there was more to the 'look' than that because several people stopped me to ask if I was a pilgrim, and two English women, rather older than me, told me that they knew I was a pilgrim by my smile, apparently it shone! An American who asked me the same question was actually staying at the Reyes Católicos and when, during the conversation that followed, I told him about the free meals for pilgrims at his hotel, his immediate reaction was 'Wow! Can I get to see that?' He was clearly thinking along the same lines as I was – something like a special table, maybe a glass-enclosed arbour in one of the courtyards, where waiters would carefully serve the ten privileged pilgrims, while hotel guests would look on in respectful silence. We could not have been further from the reality of the thing.

When I arrived at the Reyes Católicos for the first of my meals, and the white-gloved doormen realised I was not a potential paying guest, I was casually directed to make my way to the back of the huge and magnificent building. After lengthy and frustrating perambulations through a garage and up and down unmarked service stairs and tiled passages, I eventually found my way to the kitchens. The food for the guests was being prepared in one part, and laid out on a counter for the waiters to take, and very fine it all looked. The chamber maids with whom I was directed to queue, received their food from an adjacent counter. Onto my divided tray went a dollop of glutinous bean stew and one of chicken and potatoes swimming horribly in a thin yellow grease. A bread roll, apple and a glass of wine filled the remaining spaces. Then it was off again, tray in hand, down several more staircases and corridors to a nasty little white-tiled room with a bare cement floor which was reserved for this pilgrim feast.

Had there been nine others it might not have been so bad I thought, but I had the grotty little room entirely to myself, and it seemed the loneliest, most derelict moment of the entire journey. I tried the bean stew and it tasted repulsive, the chicken was exactly as it looked; even the apple was flaccid and flavourless. It was strange that in a country where food was so good and inexpensive, the first uneatable meal I was offered was the one that should have been a celebration. It left just the bread and the wine, and it was as I broke the roll in half that I suddenly knew that it was this moment that had brought the completion of the pilgrimage. Like the unnamed disciples on the road to Emmaus, I too had needed to encounter the reality of the Risen Christ. He had been there in every meeting I had had along the way, and perhaps I had known this somewhere in a remote corner of my mind. But to realise it fully had required this ordinary, everyday action in which the symbol could suddenly break free and be recognised for what it was. 'They recognised Him in the breaking of the bread.' Of course.

Little, Brown now offers an exciting range of quality titles by both established and new authors. All of the books in this series are available by faxing, or posting your order to:

Little, Brown and Company (UK) Limited,
Mail order,
P.O. Box 11,
Falmouth,
Cornwall,
TR1O 9EN
Fax: 0326-376423

Payments can be made as follows: Cheque, postal order (payable to Little, Brown Cash Sales) or by credit cards, Visa/Access/Mastercard. Do not send cash or currency. U.K. customers and B.F.P.O.; Allow £1.00 for postage and packing for the first book, plus 50p for the second book, plus 30p for each additional book up to a maximum charge of £3.00 (7 books plus). U.K. orders over £75 free postage and packing.

Overseas customers including Ireland, please allow £2.00 for postage and packing for the first book, plus £1.00 for the second book, plus 50p for each additional book.

NAME (Block Letters) ....
ADDRESS ....
....
....

☐ I enclose my remittance for ....

☐ I wish to pay by Visa/Access/Mastercard

Number ☐☐☐☐☐☐☐☐☐☐☐☐☐☐☐☐

Card Expiry Date ☐☐☐☐